北京百家精品四合院旅游指南
A Tourist Guide to 100 Refined Quadrangle Courtyards in Beijing

皇城脚下四合院

Quadrangle Courtyards by the Imperial City Walls

TOP 100

北京市东城区旅游发展委员会 编
Dongcheng District Commission of Tourism Development of Beijing Municipality

北京 旅游教育出版社
Tourism Education Press

前言 Preface

　　一座城的记忆，储存在她的建筑里。

　　北京城的记忆，储存在皇城脚下胡同深处的四合院里。

　　看那皇城脚下，大大小小的四合院，背靠背，面对面，被院落间的通道连成了串儿，织就了一条条风情万千的胡同；大大小小的胡同纵横交错，织就了一座独一无二的北京城。

　　而胡同深处，是无数温暖的家……这家的温暖，足以让一个游客驻足，流连，忘返。

　　在这里，我们选择以旅行的方式来走近四合院，感受那里的一砖一瓦带给我们的温暖与感动。也许，100家四合院不能代表京城四合院的全部，标准的四合院也越来越变得稀缺，但是，作为一个文化符号，我们触摸了它，感知了它，就已足够。

　　2013年的最后一个冬日，让我们回到小时候最熟悉的四合小院，一起聆听老胡同给我们讲从前的故事……

　　The memory of a city is stored in her buildings.

　　The memory of Beijing is stored in the quadrangle courtyards in the deep hutong by the Imperial City walls.

　　The quadrangle courtyards in various sizes stand face to face or back against back, running like the beads on the strings of the hutong. The hutongs thus become fascinating and charming. All different hutongs crisscross in the city thus present the uniqueness of Beijing.

　　In the deep ends of the hutongs, there lies numerous cozy homes. The warmth of the homes stops the tourists and makes them stay, fascinated and enchanted.

　　We would get a close look at the quadrangle courtyards by travelling, feeling the emotions brought by the bricks and tiles. The 100 quadrangle courtyards might not represent all the quadrangle courtyards in the city of Beijing, and the most traditional quadrangle courtyards have become more and more scarce. Anyhow, as a cultural symbol, we have touched it and felt it. This is enough.

　　In the last winter day of 2013, let's go back to the familiar quadrangle courtyards in our childhood and listen to the stories told by the old hutongs.

编　者

目录 Contents

印象·四合院 / 6
Impression·Quadrangle Courtyards

分区导览 / 10
Guides to the Different Areas

东皇城根沿线 / 12
Along the Foot of East Imperial City Walls

南锣鼓巷文化休闲街 / 28
Nanluoguxiang Alley Cultural Street

北锣鼓巷、鼓楼周边 / 50
Beiluoguxiang Alley, Gulou and About

雍和宫、五道营周边 / 66
Lama Temple, Wudaoying and About

北新桥周边 / 88
Beixinqiao Bridge and About

东四、灯市口周边 / 98
Dongsi, Dengshikou and About

前门周边 / 120
Qianmen and About

东城区自助旅游指南 / 129
DIY Tourist Guide To Beijing Dongcheng Distrct

索引 / 130
Index

北京市东城区旅游地图
The Tourist Map of Dongcheng District Beijing City

印象·四合院
Impression·Quadrangle Courtyards

"云开闾阖三千丈,雾暗楼台百万家。"这"百万家"的住宅,说的便是老北京的四合院。

为什么称作"四合院"呢?这是因为,四合院里的东、西、南、北都有房子,四面房屋围在一起,形成一个"口"字形的院落,即为四合院。

四合院是北京建筑的细胞,不同类型的建筑,正是由这种最基本的四合院组合而成的。其中,规模最大、形态最复杂的四合院建筑群就是皇城——紫禁城。

四合院的神髓在于一个"合"字,它将几代人"合"在了一起。就拿住房来讲,"北屋为尊,两厢次之,倒座为宾,杂屋为附",最大最敞亮的房子自然是要留给父母住的。一家人按照父慈子孝、夫唱妇随、长幼有序的家庭伦理观念和和美美地生活在一起。

The Chinese poem goes "the clear sky unveils a good view to all the gates of the houses within a radius of 10 kilometers; while the fog hides millions of the houses." The "millions of the houses" refer the quadrangle courtyards in the ancient city of Beijing.

Why did the courtyard get the name "quadrangle courtyards"? It is because in a courtyard, there are houses in all four directions, east, west, south and north. The houses from the four directions make a courtyard in the shape of square, and it is why it is called a quadrangle.

The quadrangle courtyards form the cells of the traditional buildings in Beijing, and they forms different styles of the buildings, among which the greatest and most complicated quadrangle building is the Imperial Palace, or the Forbidden City.

The Chinese word for quadrangle courtyards literally means the courtyard for harmony. "Harmony" is actually the essence of the quadrangle courtyards, for it brings several generation together harmoniously. Take the traditional accommodation for example, "the house in the north is for the most distinguished, the east and the west go next, the south house is for the guest, and the back rooms are for dependants." The biggest house is naturally for the parents and a family would live happily and harmoniously according to the traditional Chinese family ethics: filial piety, conjugal felicity and brotherly respect.

老北京过去有个顺口溜: "天棚、鱼缸、石榴树,老爷、肥狗、胖丫头",可以说是四合院生活的写照。
There is an old saying in Beijing in the past, and it goes "a canopy, a fish tank, a pomegranate tree, an old master, a fat dog and a chubby girl". That is the vivid picture of the life in the quadrangle courtyards.

四合院的结构
The Structures of Quadrangle Courtyards

正规的北京四合院一般坐落在东西方向的胡同里,坐北朝南,以中轴线贯穿。北房为正房,东西房为厢房,南房房门向北开,所以叫倒座,四面房屋各自独立,彼此间通过游廊连接起来。房屋四周再围以高墙形成四合,在宅院东南角开一个大门。

The traditional Beijing quadrangle courtyards are usually located in the Hutong of the east-west directions. It faces south and the central axis runs through it. The north house is the main house, the east and west house are the side rooms, the door to the south rooms faces north and called the opposite house. The houses on the four sides are separate but connected by corridors. There are high walls outside the four sides of the houses and the main entrance is located in the southeast corner of the courtyard.

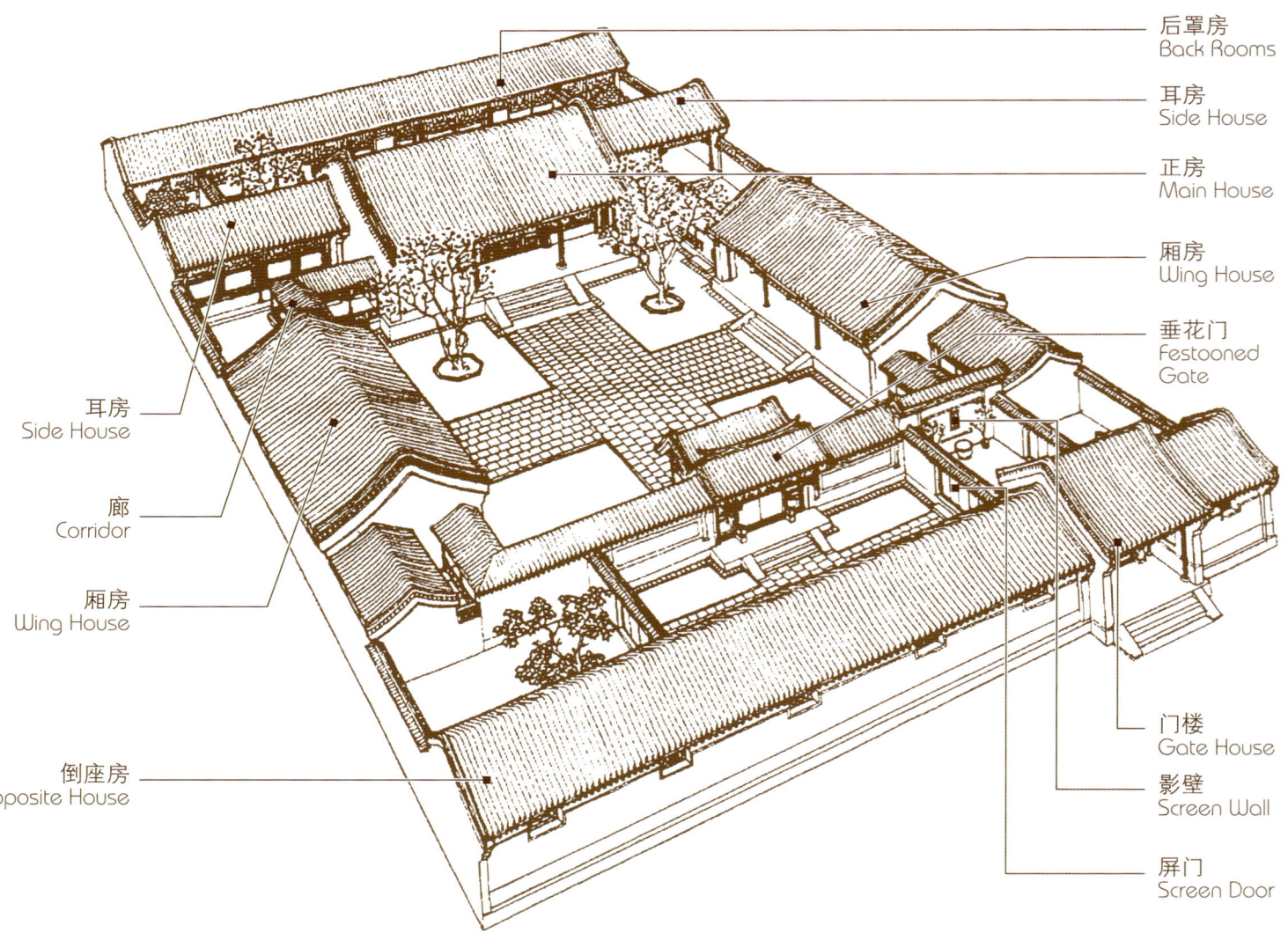

底图引自《中国古代建筑史》(刘敦桢,1984年)

门楼
Gate House: 四合院的院门都开在东南角，而不开在正中间。

The main entrances in all the courtyard are located in the southeast corner but not in the middle of the south wall.

影壁
Screen Wall: 影壁面对着大门，起到屏障的作用。按照风水学的说法，院子外面的气是邪气，院子里的气叫财气，影壁阻挡着邪气进到院子里去。在北京有两座影壁中外闻名，它们都被称为九龙壁，一是故宫九龙壁，一是北海九龙壁。

The screen wall faces the main entrance and serves as a protective screen. According to Fengshui theory, the trend outside the courtyard is considered as an evil influence, and the trend in the courtyard is wealthy influence. The screen wall could prevent the evil influence from entering the courtyard. There are two famous screen walls known to the world in Beijing, and they are all called the Nine-Dragon Screen, the one in the Imperial Palace and the other in Beihai Park.

垂花门
Festooned Gate: 以前大宅门里的女性是"大门不出，二门不迈"，这个"二门"就是垂花门。送客人不可以走出这个门。垂花门是四合院内分隔里外院的最华丽的装饰门。因其檐柱不落地，垂吊在屋檐下，其下有一垂珠，通常彩绘成花瓣的形式，故称垂花门。没有垂花门的则可用月亮门分隔内外宅。

The female members of the family living in the big Quadrangle Courtyards didn't leave the main entrance or the second gate. The second gate is the festooned gate, and the females could not step out of this gate when seeing the guests off. The festooned gate, being the most wonderful decoration, separates and communicates the outer yard and the inner yard. The eave columns do not reach the ground and hang under the eave with a ball usually painted in the pattern of the flower petals. That is why it is called the festooned gate. If there is no festooned gate, it could be replaced by the moon gate to separate the inner and outer yards.

倒座房
Opposite House: 四合院临街的南房叫做倒座房，一般是五间，房门向北开，正对着垂花门。多做客厅或书房。

The house in the south of the courtyard is called the opposite house. There are usually five rooms with the door facing north and the festooned gate which are mostly living rooms or studies.

厢房
Wing House: 四合院东西两面的房子叫厢房，由子女晚辈住。东厢房比西厢房高，细心的人们数数台阶就知道了。在中国人看来，东边为上、西边为下。所以，男孩子要在东厢房里读书，女孩子要在西厢房学习针线。

The east and west houses are called the wing houses, accommodating the young generations. The east house is usually higher than the west house, if you are very observant and would like to count the steps in from the houses. For the Chinese people, the east bears more important meaning than the west. So the boys would do reading in the east wing houses and the girls learn how to sew in the west wing houses.

正房
Main House: 四合院里坐北朝南、最高最大的房是主人房。正房的房间数不可以是双数，有四根柱子的叫五间房，有两根柱子的叫三间房。

The main house faces south and is the highest and biggest house in the courtyard. The number of the rooms in the main house could not be even numbers. The house with four columns is called five-room house and the house with two columns is called three-room house.

耳房
Side House: 正房的两侧各有一间或两间进深、高度都偏小的房间，如同挂在正房两侧的两只耳朵，故称耳房。多用来放东西。

There are one or two houses on both sides of the main house, and they are smaller and lower. They look like the ears to the main house and that is why they are called ear house in Chinese or side house in English. They usually serve as storage rooms.

后罩房
Back Rooms: 在正房后面有一排和正房平行的房屋，它在四合院的最后一进院子里，比较隐秘，一般是女儿和女佣等女眷居住之地。

At the back of the main house, there lie the back rooms in the final courtyard, which is horizontal with the main house. The back rooms are quite concealed, and accommodate the daughter and maids.

分区导览
Guides to the Different Areas

东皇城根沿线 / 12
Along the Foot of East Imperial City Walls

南锣鼓巷文化休闲街 / 28
Nanluoguxiang Alley Cultural Street

北锣鼓巷、鼓楼周边 / 50
Beiluoguxiang Alley, Gulou and About

雍和宫、五道营周边 / 66
Lama Temple, Wudaoying and About

北新桥周边 / 88
Beixinqiao Bridge and About

东四、灯市口周边 / 98
Dongsi, Dengshikou and About

前门周边 / 120
Qianmen and About

老北京的四合院是一部由砖木写就的史书
可以读出许多东西来

The quadrangle courtyards from the old Beijing is the history book written by bricks and wood that you could read a lot from it

东皇城根沿线
Along the Foot of East Imperial City Walls

  坐落在紫禁城与王府井步行街之间的皇城根遗址公园，是历史上明、清皇城根东墙的位置。从元代起，北京城由紫禁城、皇城、外城三个部分组成，最里面的是紫禁城，即现在的故宫，最外面的是外城，即现在的北京二环路一线，中间为皇城。

  如今，旧时的皇城城墙已不复存在，要想领略古都风采，唯有走到胡同深处，去叩开那一座座四合院的大门……

  The Imperial City Wall Relics Park is located between the Forbidden City and the Wangfujing Street, and it is the location of the Royal City east wall during the Ming and Qing Dynasties. From the Yuan Dynasty, the city of Beijing consists of the Forbidden City, the Royal City and the outer city. The most inside one in the middle is what we called the Imperid Palace now. The outer city lies along the second ring road, and what is between the outer city and the Forbidden City is the Royal City.

  The old Royal City wall does not exist any longer, and if you would like to take a glance at the ancient city, you have to walk into the deep hutong and knock on the doors of the conrtyards...

1. 怡尔国际商务会馆 Tiananmen Best Year Courtyard Hotel / 14
2. 天地一家 Tiandi Group / 15
3. 木棉花酒店 Hotel Kapok Beijing / 16
4. 马克南四合轩 Brian Mckenna @ The Courtyard / 17
5. 皇家驿栈·天安门店 The Emperor·Tiananmen Branch / 18
6. 老舍纪念馆 Lao She Memorial Hall / 19
7. 刘宅食府 Liu's Restaurant / 20
8. 红江湖餐厅（小云南）Hongjianghu Restaurant / 21
9. 串府 Chuanfu Restaurant / 22
10. Temple Restaurant Beijing（TRB）/ 23
11. 景山花园酒店 Jingshan Garden Hotel / 24
12. 城墙客栈 City Walls Courtyard / 25
13. 古槐苑 Scholar Tree Hotel / 26

出行提示：东皇城根沿线南有地铁1号线，北有地铁6号线。从1号线"天安门东"站出来一路向北，或从6号线"南锣鼓巷"站出来一路向南，沿着东皇城根遗址公园，边走边看，一个又一个惊喜将会等着你！

Travel Tips: There is Subway Line 1 to the south and Subway Line 6 to the north of the foot of east Imperial City walls. Go north from "Tiananmen East" Station of Subway Line 1, or go south from "Nanluoguxiang" Station of Subway Line 6. Walk through the Imperial City Wall Relics Park, and there will be surprise after surprise waiting for you!

皇城脚下四合院

怡尔国际商务会馆
Tiananmen Best Year Courtyard Hotel
在皇族禁地体味幽宅生活
To Experience the Quiet Life in the Imperial Forbidden Zones

地址 (Add)：南池子大街灯笼库胡同 1 号 / No.1 Denglongku Hutong, Nanchizi Street

电话 (Tel)：8610-6523 8501

特色 (Themed)：家庭套间四合院客房 / Courtyard Hotel with Family Suite

地铁 (Subway)：1 号线天安门东站 B 出口 / Exit B of Tiananmen East Station, Line 1

　　北京的南池子实在是个特殊的地方，它是昔日的皇族禁地，如今，寻常百姓也可以深入其中，触摸那些宠辱不惊的黄瓦灰墙。在这黄瓦灰墙掩映的灯笼库胡同，有一座叫"怡尔"的四合院宾馆。夕阳西下，坐在门口的躺椅上，望着远处高高低低的四合院屋顶，或是和书法名家来个不期而遇，岂不美哉！怡尔，正如它的英文名字"Best Year"所暗含的那样，这里"别墅风光无限，幽宅岁月常新"！

Nanchizi of Beijing is really a special place, where used to be the imperial forbidden zone, but now the ordinary people can go inside to touch and feel those yellow tiles and grey walls which went through so numerous honors and disgraces. In the Denglongku Hutong hidden among those yellow tiles and grey walls, there is located Tiananmen Best Year Courtyard Hotel. Sitting on the sling chair at the gate and looking into the distance the varied rooftops of the courtyards under the sunset, or coming across a renowned calligrapher, how wonderful it is! Best Year, as its English name indicates, enjoys the marvelous views of the villas and the new lives of the quiet courtyards.

Quadrangle Courtyards by the Imperial City Walls

天地一家
Tiandi Group
奢而不靡的时尚美食天地
The Luxury but Not Extravagant Paradise for Gourmets

皇城脚下南池子里隐藏的这方天地,正如见证过古都风貌的紫禁城一般,静立在喧嚣的长安街北侧,静观浮华,奢而不靡。从这家餐厅的每个房间望去,皇城景色尽收眼底。即便看不到皇城之美,悉心的主人也会在窗前遍植竹子,让翠绿舒展你的情怀。在二楼一侧包间的露台上,更可以看到整片皇史宬明黄的琉璃瓦屋顶。凭窗而坐,享用着精致的"清酒浸鹅肝",方知什么是天地一家!

This small place hidden in Nanchizi at the foot of the Imperial City Walls, as if it is the same as the Forbidden City witnessed the history of the old metropolis, quietly stands in the north of the busy Chang'an Avenue, and silently observes the vanity of the city. The restaurant is luxury but not extravagant. Looked at the Imperial City from every room of the restaurant, you will have a panoramic view. Even though you may not see the beauty of the Imperial City, the thoughtful keeper plants bamboos everywhere in front of the windows, to let the green limber up your feelings. At the balcony of the compartment room on one side of the 2nd floor, you can see the whole picture of the Imperial Archival Vault's glaze-tiled yellow roof. Sitting by the window and enjoying the exquisite "Sake-soaked Goose's Liver", you will get to know what restaurant Tiandi Group is!

地址 (Add): 南池子大街 140 号 /No.140, Nanchizi Street
电话 (Tel): 8610-8511 5556
特色 (Themed): 京菜、鲁菜、港式火锅 / Beijing Cuisine, Shandong Cuisine, Hong Kong Style hotpot
地铁 (Subway): 1 号线天安门东站 B 出口 /Exit B of Tiananmen East Station, Line 1

皇城脚下四合院

木棉花酒店
Hotel Kapok Beijing
故宫旁的空中庭院
The Aerial Garden Next to the Forbidden City

  北京的城市肌理并不仅仅在黄瓦灰墙间，故宫东华门外，有一个充满传统文化气息的现代生活空间，它用灯笼、格栅这些中国传统的建筑饰品，给酒店这个冰冷的建筑赋予了鲜活的生命，就连故宫，也透过这些格栅，成为了酒店肌理的一部分。化整为零的垂直院落系统，让16个满眼春色的空中庭院奏响了最为动听的中国传统建筑旋律。传统、时尚、简约、高雅，这就是木棉花酒店。

The texture of Beijing city is not limited to the yellow tiles and grey walls. Outside of the east gate of the Forbidden City, there lies a modern life space immersed with the traditional culture. It uses such Chinese traditional architectural ornaments as the lanterns and grilles, and endows the cold architecture of the restaurant with vivid life. And through these grilles, even the Forbidden City becomes a part of the hotel texture. The vertical courtyard system, which breaks up the whole into parts, let these 16 colorful aerial gardens play the most beautiful melody of the Chinese traditional architecture. That is Hotel Kapok Beijing, which is full of tradition, fashion, simplicity and elegance.

地址 (Add)：东华门大街 16 号 /16 Donghuamen Street
电话 (Tel)：8610-6525 9988
特色 (Themed)：京菜、川菜、庭院客房 / Beijing Cuisine, Sichuan Cuisine, Courtyard Guestrooms
地铁 (Subway)：1号线天安门东站 B 出口 /Exit B of Tiananmen East Station, Line 1

马克南四合轩
Brian Mckenna @ The Courtyard
中西合璧的现代料理店
A Modern Restaurant with Both Chinese and Western Foods

当大不列颠的顶级西餐大厨遇上中国紫禁城,将会演绎出怎样的传统与时尚大戏?故宫东华门外、筒子河边,大幕徐徐拉开,亚洲顶级食材和香料,经名厨马克南之手,与地中海风味相碰撞,带着食客们的味蕾在一道道中西合璧的现代料理中旅行,最极致的创新味觉体验就此开始。餐后,来上一杯马克南独创的特调鸡尾酒,或点上一支主厨钦点的雪茄,在雪茄堂遥望皇宫护城河,至尊体验由此开始。

When the chef of Britain's top western-style food comes across the Forbidden City of China, how could he deduce the tradition and fashion show? Outside the east gate and along the moat of the Forbidden City, there opens the grand curtain: as Asian top cuisine material and spices run into Mediterranean flavors through Mckenna's hand, and travel with the diners' taste buds in the modern cuisines with a combination of Chinese and western cuisines styles, the ultimate experience of the innovated taste begins. After dinner, you may order a cup of cocktail specially mixed by Mckenna, or light a chef named cigar recommended by the chef, and look afar to the moat of the Imperial Palace in the cigar hall. An extreme experience begins.

地址 (Add): 东华门大街 95 号 /95 ,Donghuamen Street
电话 (Tel): 8610-6526 8883
特色 (Themed): 创意欧洲菜 /Creative European Cuisine
地铁 (Subway): 1 号线天安门东站 C 出口 /Exit C of Tiananmen East Station, Line 1
网址 (Website): www.bmktc.com

皇城脚下四合院

皇家驿栈·天安门店
The Emperor · Tiananmen Branch
可以俯瞰紫禁城的家外之家
The House Beyond the House Which Can Overlook the Forbidden City

  与大清皇帝的寝宫乾清宫仅一墙之隔的，是皇家驿栈天安门店。下榻于此，时隐时现的皇家城墙与客房家具融为一体，让你穿梭在不同的时空中，看尽人间浮华，回归生活本真。邀三五好友围坐在"玻璃坊"食餐厅的落地飘窗前，远望景山公园，相信你早已忘了杯中酒的滋味。夕阳西下，在天台"饮"吧赏"升灯"，俯瞰落日的余晖肆意地洒在皇城金色的屋顶上，一种君临天下的感觉将油然而生。

  Separated by the wall of Palace of Heavenly Purity the chamber of The Qing Dynasty is the Emperor · Tiananmen Branch. Alighting at this hotel, where the imperial walls come and go and are combined with the furniture of the hotel rooms, you will shuttle between the different spaces, see all the vanities of the world, and return to the truth of life. To invite a couple of good friends to sit around before the French bay windows of the Glass Workshop restaurant, and look afar to the Jingshan Park, you may, I believe, have forgotten the relish of the wine. At the sunset, to enjoy the lantern rising at the Beverage Bar on the balcony, and overlook the glow of the sunset wantonly shedding on the golden roofs of the Imperial City, you will naturally have a feeling that the sovereign descends the world.

地址(Add)：骑河楼街33号/33, Qihelou Street

电话(Tel)：8610-6526 5566

特色(Themed)：创意菜、新古典中国菜、时尚客房/Innovative Cuisine, New Classical Chinese Cuisine, Stylish Guestrooms

地铁(Subway)：1号线天安门东站B出口/Exit B of Tiananmen East Station, Line 1

网址（Website）：www.theemperor.com.cn

老舍纪念馆
Lao She Memorial Hall
胡同里的文化记忆
The Memory of Culture in Hutong

地址 (Add)：灯市口西街丰富胡同 19 号 /19,Fengfu Hutong, Dengshikou West Street
电话 (Tel)：8610-6559 9218
特色 (Themed)：名人故居 / Former Residence of the Celebrity Laoshe
地铁 (Subway)：5 号线灯市口 A 出口 /Exit A of Dengshikou, Line 5
网址（Website）：www.bjlsjng.com

  皇城有的不只是浮华，在离东皇城根南街不远的丰富胡同里，隐匿着一个小四合院，院子的主人在这里生活了 16 年之久，创作出了《茶馆》《四世同堂》等不朽的作品，周总理、曹禺等人曾在这个院子里留下过足迹，这里就是人民艺术家老舍的故居，现在的老舍纪念馆。若想凭吊这位有着卓越才华的老人，一定要到这里转转，因为，一个"文艺尽责的小卒"，曾生活在这里。

  The Imperial City does not have the ostentation only. There is a small courtyard in Fengfu Hutong not far from the south street of East Imperial City Walls, where the owner of the courtyard lived for 16 years, and wrote many immortal works such as *Tea House* and *Four Generation under One Roof*. People like Premier Zhou and Cao Yu paid visit to this house. That is the former residence of Lao She the people's artist, and now Lao She Memorial Hall. If you would like to pay your respect to this outstanding capable old man, you should come here to have a look, because here ever lived a "literarily responsible cipher".

刘宅食府
Liu's Restaurant
老北京人"记忆里寻找"的地儿
A Place For Old Beijinese to Search For in the Memory

　　沿着东皇城根南街一路向北，在美术馆东门蒋家大院胡同内，有一个古老的四合院，远远地，就能闻见烤鸭炉里飘来的果木香，这里就是刘宅食府，经营地道的宫廷小吃以及有些将要失传的老北京名菜。灰砖雕花的影壁，瓦缸里游戏的金鱼以及红色窗花……无一不在告诉你：这儿是老北京人"记忆里寻找"的地儿；这儿是外地人所说的"特北京"的地儿；这儿是外国人所说的"真正北京"的地儿。

All the way up to the north along the south street of East Imperial City Walls, an old courtyard is located in the Jiangjia Dayuan Hutong at the east gate of the Art Gallery. You may smell, far from the distance, the fruit-wood fragrance from the roast-duck stove. That's Liu's Restaurant, which offers veritable imperial snacks and some would-be lost old Beijing renowned dishes. The grey brick carved screen wall, the golden fish frolicking in the vat, the red window flowers, and so on, all tell you that this is a place which the old Beijineses are looking for in their memory, this is a place that the outsiders call the typical Beijing, and this is a place that the foreigners call the real Beijing.

地址 (Add)：美术馆东街蒋家大院胡同 8 号 /8 Jiangjiadayuan Hutong, Meishuguan East Street

电话 (Tel)：8610-6400 5912

特色 (Themed)：北京菜（北京烤鸭、醋焖多宝鱼、刘宅茄子卷）Beijing Cuisine (Roast Duck, Braised Turbot, Liu's Eggplant Rolls)

地铁 (Subway)：5 号、6 号线东四站 E 出口 /Exit E of Dongsi Station, Line 5 or 6

网址 (Website)：www.bjliuzhaishifu.com

红江湖餐厅（小云南）
Hongjianghu Restaurant
火红的锅子，红火的日子
The Flaming Pot and the Flourishing Life

红江湖，相信看到这几个字的食客们一定们会把它和辣椒联系在一起。没错，这里就是经营正宗云南菜的传说中的红江湖。它在东皇城根北街美术馆西侧一个亮着"小云南"招牌的四合院里，各种红油火锅、麻辣耗儿鱼及云南大理酸辣乌江鱼，让你经受一次次麻辣诱惑。火红的灯笼，火红的锅子，把老北京风情的四合院装扮得红红火火。

I am sure that when diners see Hongjianghu, they will combine these characters with the hot pepper. That's right this restaurant is the legendary Hongjianghu which produces the authentic Yunnan dishes. The restaurant is situated in a courtyard, where a facia writes Little Yunnan, in the North Street of East Imperial City Walls to the west side of the Art Gallery. The restaurant serves various spicy hotpots, peppered and chilli leather jacket, and sour and spicy Wujiang River fish of Yunnan Dali, and entices you to experience the peppered and hot tastes one time after another. The flaming lanterns and pots warmly decorates the courtyard with old Beijing fashion.

地址 (Add)：东皇城根北街 28 号 /28 Donghuanchenggen North Street
电话 (Tel)：8610-6401 9498
特色 (Themed)：大理酸辣乌江鱼 /Dali Hot and Sour Fish from Wujiang River
地铁 (Subway)：6 号线南锣鼓巷站 A 出口 /Exit A of Nanluoguxiang Station, Line 6

皇城脚下四合院

串府
Chuanfu Restaurant
美味与四合院连成串儿
The Delicacies and the Courtyards Cluster Together

当人们把路边的烤串儿搬到密闭的四合院里，在青砖灰瓦、雕梁画栋、装修古典的院子里大快朵颐的时候，那将产生怎样的餐饮冲击波。东皇城根北街的这家"串府"餐厅，可谓独辟蹊径。无论是肉质细腻的深海鳕鱼，还是那经过炭烤的鲜美乳鸽，都是闻一闻都会口水直流的菜品。串府串起的不光是皇城文化的大气，更有寻常百姓的人气！

As people move the roadside kebabs into the enclosed courtyard, and glut themselves with delicacies in the courts which are decorated with grey bricks and tiles, carved beams and painted rafters and in a classical style, what shock wave will it result in? The Chuanfu Restaurant located at the North Street of East Imperial City Walls develops its own style. Both the deep sea codfish with delicate meat and the delicious young pigeons roasted with charcoal are dishes which could make your mouth slobber as soon as you smell. What is clustered together here is not only the magnificence of the Imperial City's culture, but also the vogue of the ordinary people.

地址 (Add)： 美术馆东街隆福医院北 20 米 /20m North of Longfu Hospital, Meishuguan East Street

电话 (Tel)： 8610-6422 0055

特色 (Themed)： 烧烤 /Barbeque

地铁 (Subway)： 地铁 5 号线东四站 E 出口 /Exit E of Dongsi Station, Line 5

Temple Restaurant Beijing (TRB)
敕建寺庙里的欧式西餐生产线
The European-style Western Food Production Line in the Temple Constructed by the Imperial Order

御用印经厂、藏传佛教圣地、黑白电视机、欧式西餐厅……这些看似毫不相干的东西,在故宫东北角、景山东沿、北河沿街区曲折蜿蜒的胡同中,找到了它们共同的归宿。把它们紧紧联系在一起的,是有着600多年历史的"敕建智珠寺群"。这个曾经的御用印经厂,一度被用作生产黑白电视机的厂房,如今,又变成了欧式西餐生产线。常变常新的菜单,由TRB资深侍酒师悉心打造的"诱惑"酒单,令挑剔的食客惊喜连连。

Such seemingly unrelated things as the royal scripture-printing factory, the holy land of Tibetan Buddhism, the black and white TV, and European style western food restaurant find their common destiny in the serpentine Hutongs at the northeast corner of the Forbidden City, along the east streets of Jingshan Hill and the streets of Beiheyan. What tightly binds them together is the Zhizhu Temple Compound which was built by the imperial order with a history of over 600 years. The former royal scripture-printing factory used to be utilized as a black and white TV factory, but now becomes a European style western food production line. The timely innovated menu and the alluring wine list carefully created by the TRB senior sommelier will make the picky eaters surprise.

地址 (Add):沙滩北街 23 号 /23 Shatan North Street
电话 (Tel):8610-8400 2232
特色 (Themed):欧式西餐厅、葡萄酒晚宴、鸡尾酒晚宴
European Western Restaurant, Wine Banquet, Cocktail Banquet
地铁 (Subway):6 号线南锣鼓巷站 B 出口 /Exit B of Nanluoguxiang Station, Line 6
网址 (Website):www.temple-restaurant.com

皇城脚下四合院

景山花园酒店
Jingshan Garden Hotel
景山公园的后花园
The Back Garden of Jingshan Park

　　景山花园酒店，堪称景山公园的后花园，与这座元、明、清三代皇家园林公园仅咫尺之遥。也许是厌倦了城市的喧嚣，这处古朴典雅的庭院酒店选择用安静恬淡来坚守那份至简至美，露天庭院一步一景，不负其花园酒店的美名。坐在庭院中，偷得浮生半日闲，沏一壶茶，看池中鱼儿慵懒地游戏，整个人也会自然而然放松下来。

Jingshan Garden Hotel could be called as the back garden of Jingshan Park, and is adjacent to this royal garden park of the Yuan, Ming and Qing Dynasties. It might be tired of the city's clamor, and this simple and elegant garden restaurant chooses quietness and indifference to maintain ultimate simplicity and beauty. The outdoor garden and court feature one scene for each step, which lives up to its fame as a garden hotel. Sitting in the garden to take a break from the busy work, infusing a pot of tea, and admiring the fish indolently frolicking in the pond, you will relax yourself completely.

地址 (Add)：景山东街三眼井胡同 68 号 /68 Sanyanjing Hutong, Jingshan East Street
电话 (Tel)：8610-8404 7979
特色 (Themed)：四合院客房 /Courtyard Guestrooms
地铁 (Subway)：1 号线天安门东站 C 出口，换乘 5 路公交车至景山东街 Exit C of Tiananmen East Station, Line 1, Then Transfer to Bus 5 to Jingshan East Street Station

城墙客栈
City Walls Courtyard Inn
皇城边上寻找北京记忆
To Find the Memory of Beijing at the Imperial City Walls

城墙客栈，一个依托北京古都中轴线及故宫、景山建筑群而走进人们视野的四合小院酒店，一如它的名字那样亲民、质朴。朱漆的大门、安详的兵马俑及高悬的宫灯，这些中国元素再配上皇城脚下寻常百姓安闲的生活画面，你想不来，都难。

City Walls Courtyard is a small courtyard inn, which comes into the people's eyes by relying on the central line of Beijing old capital and the Forbidden City as well as Jingshan construction complex. It is as amiable and primitive as its name. Such Chinese factors as red-varnished gate, the serene Terra-Cotta Warriors and highly hanged lanterns as well as the ease life picture of the ordinary people at the Imperial City Walls are irresistible, and it is very difficult for you not to come.

地址 (Add)：碾子胡同 57 号 / 57 Nianzi Hutong
电话 (Tel)：8610-6402 7805
特色 (Themed)：四合院特色客房 / Courtyard Guestrooms
地铁 (Subway)：6 号线南锣鼓巷站 A 出口 / Exit A of Nanluoguxiang Station, Line 6
网址 (Website)：www.beijingcitywalls.com

皇城脚下四合院

古槐苑
Scholar Tree Hotel
听老槐树诉说皇城故事
Listen to the Old Scholar Tree to Tell About the Story of the Imperial City

　　古槐苑，一个有着600多年历史的明代庭院，曾为紫禁城大内禁地二十四局所属，隐匿在景山公园以北众多世界级景点中，在喧嚣的城市中守望着那段专属于自己的岁月。如今的古槐苑，已变身成雅致的四合院酒店，为钟情于老北京皇城文化的人精心营造了一个歇脚的驿站和心灵的港湾。来过这儿的人，一定会流连于院内那几株古槐，在暮鼓晨钟间，看沧海桑田，观城市变迁。

Scholar Tree Hotel has a court of the Ming Dynasty with a history of over 600 years, where used to belong to the 24-bureau of the Imperial Palace in the Forbidden City. It is hidden in the world class scenic spots to the north of Jingshan Park, and keeps in the busy city its own years. Scholar Tree Hotel today has been transformed into an elegant courtyard hotel, and elaborately created a rest stage and a spiritual hub for those who love the culture of the Imperial City of the old Beijing. Those who have been here are bound to be fond of the old scholar trees in this Hotel to look into the vicissitudes of the history and observe the great change of the city during the evening drums and morning bells in the monastery.

地址 (Add)：地安门内大街锥把胡同1号 /1 Zhuiba Hutong, Di'anmen Street

电话 (Tel)：订餐(Catering)8610-6401 1583 订房(Room) 8610-6400 6668

特色 (Themed)：河北菜系、官家布局特色客房、河北特色商品 / Hebe Cuisine, Featured Guestrooms, Hebei Special Goods

地铁 (Subway)：6号线南锣鼓巷站 A 出口 /Exit A of Nanluoguxiang Station, Line 6

Quadrangle Courtyards by the Imperial City Walls

南锣鼓巷文化休闲街
Nanluoguxiang Alley Cultural Street

　　南锣鼓巷，南北走向，北起鼓楼东大街，南止地安门东大街，全长786米，宽8米，与元大都（1267年）同期建成，是我国唯一完整保存着元代胡同院落肌理、规模最大、品级最高、资源最丰富的棋盘式传统民居区。

　　如今的南锣鼓巷，已被打造成了文化休闲一条街，成为了北京的文化符号，帝都的小纽约。

Nanluoguxiang Alley is north and south bound, and it starts from Gulou East Street, and ends at Di'anmen East Street. It is 786 meters long and 8 meters wide, and it was constructed in 1267 when the Yuan Dadu was constructed. Nanluoguxiang Alley is the only traditional residential area that keeps everything of the hutong and courtyand system from the Yuan Dynasty. It is the largest and best traditional residential area in the pattern of the Chinese chess board with the most colorful resources.

Nanluoguxiang Alley has now been remodeled into the cultural street, becoming a cultural symbol of Beijing, the mini New York of the Capital.

14. 都江源 Source / 30
15. 侣松园宾馆 Lvsongyuan Hotel / 31
16. 十八茶膳 18 Garden / 32
17. 红宝鼎 Hongbaoding Restaurant / 33
18. 呫摸餐吧 Taste Restaurant / 34
19. 蓬蒿剧场 Penghao Theatre · Cafe / 35
20. 江湖酒吧 Jianghu Bar / 36
21. 涵珍园国际酒店 Han's Royal Garden / 37
22. 束河人家 House of Shuhe / 38
23. 杜革四合院酒店 DuGe Courtyard Boutique Hotel / 39
24. 16毫米酒吧 16mm Bar / 40
25. 创可贴T恤 Plastered T-shirts / 41
26. 紫地客栈 Purple Courtyard / 42
27. 文宇奶酪 Wenyu Cheese / 43
28. 茅盾故居 Former Residence of Mao Dun / 44
29. 古韵坊怡景酒店 MU HOTEL / 45
30. 古巷贰拾号商务会所 Beijing Guxiang 20 Hotel / 46
31. 秦唐府七号院 Courtyard 7 / 47
32. 胡同仁庭院酒店 Hutongren Courtyard Hotel / 48
33. 得着小馆 Dezhe Restaurant / 49

出行提示：元朝人设计的胡同，可供一辆马车通行，所以您去南锣鼓巷，尽量以步代车，一来人流量大，二来没地方停车，坐地铁6号线，"南锣鼓巷"站A口或B口出来，过马路即到，方便又环保。

Travel Tips: The hutong was designed in the Yuan Dynasty, so that it could allow one horse carriage to go through. When you visit the hootorg, please walk because there are many tourists and no parking lot. Take Subway Line 6 to the "Nanluoguxiang" Station, and walk across the street from Exit A or B. That will make a convenient and environmental friendly trip to the hutong.

皇城脚下四合院

都江源
Source
金庸题名的王爷府私房菜餐厅
Royal Private Kitchen Restaurant Autographed by Dr Jin Yong

　　南锣鼓巷南口右手边的两条胡同——炒豆胡同和板厂胡同可是大有来头，清末大将军蒙古亲王僧格林沁的王府就曾纵跨这两条胡同。眼前这个金庸题名的"都江源"四合院就是王府的一部分。大门口没有任何关于这是一处餐厅的标志，只有一块黑匾上写着墨绿色的店名。斯人已去，荫蔽着院子的那棵百年枣树仿佛在告诉人们，这是一个有历史、有故事的院子。

Chaodou Hongtong and Banchang Hongtong to the right of the south entrance of Nanluoguxiang Alley cannot be taken lightly in history. The residence of Mongolian Prince Sengelingin, General of the late Qing Dynasty, was located athwart these two Hutongs. "Source", the courtyard with its name autographed by Dr Jin Yong, was part of the royal mansion. No sign of a restaurant but only a black tablet with the name "Source" is hung on the top of the front door. The hundred years old jujube tree shades the yard and tells people: this is a courtyard with history and stories.

地址（Add）：南锣鼓巷板厂胡同 14 号 /14 Banchang Hutong, Nanluoguxiang Alley
电话（Tel）：8610-6400 3736
特色（Themed）：四合院私房菜 /Courtyard Private Home Cuisine
地铁（Subway）：6 号线南锣鼓巷站 A 出口 /Exit A of Nanluoguxiang Station, Line 6

Quadrangle Courtyards by the Imperial City Walls

侣松园宾馆
Lvsongyuan Hotel
僧家祠堂上的宾馆
Hotel Uprose from an Ancestral Hall

地址 (Add)：南锣鼓巷板厂胡同 22 号 /22 Banchang Hutong, Nanluoguxiang Alley
电话 (Tel)：8610-6404 0436
特色 (Themed)：四合院餐饮、住宿 / Courtyard Catering and Accommodation
地铁 (Subway)：6 号线南锣鼓巷站 A 出口 / Exit A of Nanluoguxiang Station, Line 6

醉卧沙场君莫笑，古来征战几人回！炒豆胡同和板厂胡同西口原是僧格林沁家祭祀祖先的祠堂，距紫禁城仅一箭之遥，自打征战的人儿覆没沙场后，家道中落的后代只得变卖家产，让这里成为了京华烟云。如今，在祠堂原址上兴建起了侣松园宾馆，由五个院落组成的小院正用它的恬静优雅告诉人们：岁月静好，现世安稳。

"Please don't laugh at those warriors drunk themselves, who knows how many lucky ones will survive from the wars?" The west ends of Chaodou Hutong and Banchang Hongtong, a stone's throw away from the Forbidden City, was originally the ancestral hall of Sengelinge, General of the late Qing Dynasty. The ancestors extinguished during the wars, the family fortunes declined, the later generations had to sell up properties. The hall is now remodeled as Lvsongyuan Hotel with five compounds. With its peace and elegance, the building is saying: May the life peaceful and the time tranquil.

皇城脚下四合院

十八茶膳
18 Garden
当日本料理遇上中国茶
When Japanese Cuisine Meets Chinese Tea

  与侣松园宾馆相望的是十八茶膳，这里自然也是僧格林沁宅邸的一部分。院主黄安希子是日本著名茶人，嗜爱中国本源的茶文化。中国的茶文化加上地道的日式精品餐，于是就有了十八茶膳这个名号。从来佳茗似佳人，浓妆淡抹总相宜。玲珑小院，四方独立空间，一帘幽梦，让你的南锣鼓巷之行回味无穷。

Facing Lusongyuan Hotel, 18 Garden is also part of Prince Sengelinge's mansion. The landlord now is Ms Akiko Ko, a Japanese tea master. 18 Garden is a mixture of Chinese tea culture and Japanese cuisine. Nice tea is just like the beauty, always charming either richly adorned or plainly dressed. Detached, exquisite courtyard, with fantasies behind the pearly curtain, will make your trip to Nanluoguxiang Alley interesting and meaningful.

地址 (Add)：南锣鼓巷板厂胡同 18 号 /18 Banchang Hutong, Nanluoguxiang Alley
电话 (Tel)：8610-6406 0918
特色 (Themed)：上乘精品茶，意式、日式精品餐 / Finest Quality Tea, Italian and Japanese Cuisine
地铁 (Subway)：6 号线南锣鼓巷站 A 出口 /Exit A of Nanluoguxiang Station, Line 6

Quadrangle Courtyards by the Imperial City Walls

红宝鼎 Hongbaoding Restaurant
创意美食小院儿
A Creative Cate Yard

南锣鼓巷南口左手边，大红灯笼高高挂，红底烫金的招牌把人引领进了一个创意美食小院儿。这里由麻辣香锅餐厅的主厨亲自掌勺，烹制地道纯正的四川特色烤鱼和麻辣香锅，让你在时尚风情老街，体验一把四合小院里红得够火、辣得够艳的生活。

On the left side of the south entrance of Nanluoguxiang Alley, red lanterns are risen. The red signboard with bronzing attracts people to a creative cate yard. With the genuine Sichuan grilled fish and spicy pot, the chef brings you to the hot and glamorous yard life in the ancient fascinating lane.

地址 (Add)： 南锣鼓巷 149 号 /149 Nanluoguxiang Alley
电话 (Tel)： 8610-84018856
特色 (Themed)： 京菜、川菜 / Beijing Cuisine, Sichuan Cuisine
地铁 (Subway)： 6 号线南锣鼓巷站 A 出口 / Exit A of Nanluoguxiang Station, Line 6

皇城脚下四合院

呃摸餐吧
Taste Restaurant
呃摸餐吧里呃摸北京味儿
Taste Beijing in the Taste Restaurant

　　如果老北京的味儿你还没有呃摸够，就到南锣鼓巷街口的这座小楼继续呃摸吧。它历经沧桑，幽隽高雅，既彰显皇城风范，又不乏西方韵味。在古朴得充满质感的小楼里入座，尝一尝中西合璧的宫保鸡丁比萨，再来一杯五彩呃摸鸡尾酒，看时尚风情街里的红男绿女，这生活咋就越呃摸越有味儿。

If you want more taste on Beijing, just come to this lodge in Nanluoguxiang Alley. Standing quietly and elegantly through the vicissitude of time, the lodge shows a Chinese royal city style mixed with western lingering charm. Take a seat in the lodge, have a taste of the East-West mingling style Kung Pao Chicken Pizza, with a colorful Taste cocktail, you will taste more taste of the beautiful life.

地址 (Add)：南锣鼓巷 106 号院 /106 Nanluoguxiang Alley

电话 (Tel)：8610-6401 7029

特色 (Themed)：烤鸭比萨、宫保鸡丁比萨 / Beijing Roast Duck Pizza, Kung Pao Chicken Pizza

地铁 (Subway)：6 号线南锣鼓巷站 A 出口 / Exit A of Nanluoguxiang Station, Line 6

网址（Website）：www.zamozamo.com.cn

Quadrangle Courtyards by the Imperial City Walls

蓬蒿剧场
Penghao Theatre · Cafe
北京第一家民间小剧场
The First Folk Theatre in Beijing

"仰天长笑出门去，我辈岂是蓬蒿人！"一群普通人，为了让更多的普通人走进剧场，在南锣鼓巷"中央戏剧学院"附近的这间民国四合院里，用心经营着属于大众的梦剧场。来这里，不仅是观看戏剧，也能创作戏剧；不仅是解构戏剧，更能像解构戏剧那样解构我们的人生，使它达到无限丰富的可能性。

Penghao People, originated from a poetry of the great Chinese poet Li Bai, have a figurative meaning of ordinary people. Here in a courtyard in Nanluoguxiang Alley, just nearby the Central Academy of Drama, a few ordinary people opened and operate this folk theatre for the dream of letting more ordinary people walk into theatres. In here you will not only see a drama, but also produce a drama; not only analyze a drama, but also analyze our lives and make the lives with more possibilities.

地址 (Add)：东棉花胡同 35 号 / 35 Dongmianhua Hutong
电话 (Tel)：8610-6400 6472
特色 (Themed)：希腊沙拉、烤墨西哥夹饼、自制肉酱面、胡萝卜蛋糕、精彩的话剧表演 /Greek Salad, Taco, Meat Paste, Carrot Cake, Great Play
地铁 (Subway)：6 号线南锣鼓巷站 A 出口 /Exit A of Nanluoguxiang Station, Line 6
网址（Website）：penghaotheatre.com

皇城脚下四合院

江湖酒吧
Jianghu Bar
原创音乐四合院酒吧
Original Music Courtyard Bar

这个江湖为你存在！烛光摇曳中，几株植物斜斜地靠在有些年头的墙壁上，陈年的木椅，鲜活的面孔，来自五湖四海的人，用自己的语言、自己的音乐演绎着自己心中的那个江湖传奇。你在，四合院在，音乐在，朋友就在。

This Jianghu Bar exists specially for you! In the flickering candle light, a couple of plants agley lean against the old wall. The crusted wooden chairs, fresh faces and people from all over the world deduce their own legendary stories in their own languages and music. As long as you are here, the courtyard is here, the music is here and the friends are here.

地址 (Add)：交道口南大街东棉花胡同 7 号
　　　　　　7 Dongmianhua Hutong, Jiaodaokou South Street
电话 (Tel)：8610-6401 5269
特色 (Themed)：原创音乐演出酒吧 / Original Music Performance Bar
地铁 (Subway)：6 号线南锣鼓巷站 B 出口 / Exit B of Nanluoguxiang Station, Line 6

涵珍园国际酒店
Han's Royal Garden
涵珍蕴玉的精品酒店
Refined Hotel Containing Precious Items

画眉鸣声玲珑婉转，树木百年苍劲悍然，朱红漆柱沥粉油彩，秦老胡同内别有洞天。信步于俯仰即见景山北海的一池三山，昔日烟花织锦绣，莺燕唱生平的皇都内地、清朝北兵马司将军府，如今的涵珍园国际酒店，采用中国传统的造园技术，石雕砖镂碧水玉桥，磨砖对缝沥粉贴金，处处彰显雍容宏广的王府气概。名贵字画，紫檀花梨家私，件件珍品蕴涵院中，是为"涵珍园"之意所在。下榻于此，您将在丝竹悠扬、红木幽香中享受帝王般的非凡礼遇。

The thrush's song is exquisite and sweet, the 100-year old trees grow vigorously and outrageously, red-varnished columns drip pink paints, and inside Qinlao Hutong is an altogether different world. Leisurely walk at Di'anmen, and look up and down, you will see a pond and three hills of Jingshan and Beihai, where used to be the extravagant inner palace of the imperial capital and the general mansion of the North Binmasi of the Qing Dynasty, but now is Han's Royal Garden Hotel, adopting the traditional Chinese gardening techniques such as stone carving and brick engraving, blue water and jade bridge, rubbed brick work and gelled patterning and gilding. Everywhere of the hotel apparently shows the magnificence of the distinguished royal mansion. Each precious item such as valuable calligraphy and paintings, rosewood and padauk furniture is well stored in this hotel, and it means containing precious items. To stay at this hotel, you will receive a special courtesy as a king in an atmosphere of the melodious string and wind music and the deep fragrance of the rosewood.

地址 (Add)： 南锣鼓巷秦老胡同 20 号 /20 Qinlao Hutong, Nanluoguxiang Alley
电话 (Tel)： 8610-8402 5588
特色 (Themed)： 御膳、宫廷菜、养生菜及各类西式餐饮、西式豪华套房、中式套房 /Royal Cuisine, Tonic Foods and Western Cuisine; Western Style Luxury Suite, Chinese style suite
地铁 (Subway)： 6 号线南锣鼓巷站 A 出口 /Exit A of Nanluoguxiang Station, Line 6
网址 (Website) ： www.hansroyalgarden.com

皇城脚下四合院

束河人家
House of Shuhe
好吃好玩儿又不贵
Tasty, Amusing, Affordable

　　束河古镇，云南丽江高峰之下的村寨，茶马古道上的集镇。如今，我们不仅把美丽的束河古镇带回了北京，而且把地道的云南料理也带回了北京！这就是束河人家！坐落于京城胡同深处的四合院，经营的却是世外桃源般的云南自助小火锅。小胡同里也能找到丽江的感觉。

Shuhe ancient town by the foot of the mountain in Lijiang, Yunnan Province, was a town on the ancient Tea-horse Road. "House of Shuhe" brings to Beijing not only the beauty of the ancient town but also genuine Yunnan cuisine! Serving Yunnan small hotpot in the courtyard, "House of Shuhe" gives you a feeling of Lijiang in this small hutong in Beijing.

地址 (Add)：南锣鼓巷北兵马司胡同 17 号 /17 Beibingmasi Hutong, Nanluoguxiang Alley
电话 (Tel)：8610-5721 8898 / 8404 8817
特色 (Themed)：云南火锅 /Yunnan Hotpot
地铁 (Subway)：6 号线南锣鼓巷站 A 出口 /Exit A of Nanluoguxiang Station, Line 6

杜革四合院酒店
DuGe Courtyard Boutique Hotel
胡同里的奢华世界
A Luxurious Place in the Hutong

地址（Add）：南锣鼓巷前圆恩寺胡同 26 号 /26 Qianyuan'ensi Hutong, Nanluoguxiang

电话（Tel）：8610-6406 0686

特色（Themed）：官府私家菜，中西合璧特色客房 /Royal Cuisine, Themed Guestrooms with a Combination of Chinese and Western Elements

地铁（Subway）：6 号线南锣鼓巷站 A 出口 /Exit A of Nanluoguxiang Station, Line 6

网址（Website）：www.dugecourtyard.com

红蓝相间的大门个性十足，墙脚下的烛灯把人引入了月亮门，院子里竹影婆娑，琴瑟和鸣，一曲高山流水，让人驻足窗前。客房里，水晶灯下，牡丹绚烂地绽放在玻璃墙上……当时尚女性杜革瞥见南锣鼓巷里的这一处院子时，就有了眼前这座美得让人无法呼吸的四合院。它的前世，就是18世纪落成的清朝三代大臣的府邸——索家花园的一部分。

The front door is red alternating with blue. The candle lamps lead guests into the moon gate. In the yard, the bamboo branches cast dappled shadows, now dark, now pale. A beautiful Chinese melody attracts the ears of the visitors. Under the crystal lamp in the guestroom, peony is blooming on the glass wall... The yard is made breathtaking beautifully by Du Ge, a fashionable lady, after a glimpse of it in Nanluoguxiang Alley. The preexistence of the courtyard – Suo's Garden, was a mansion built in the 18th century where lived three generations of Minister Suo in the Qing Dynasty. The courtyard is only a small part of the mansion.

16 毫米酒吧
16mm Bar
在胶片里与自己对话
Dialogue with Oneself in the Film

16 毫米，一个神奇的长度单位，人们将无限大的世界浓缩在用它丈量的胶片里……打开它，就打开了记忆的大门。当下，记忆的大门在南锣鼓巷的一家酒吧里打开，店面醒目的电影胶片 LOGO 告诉你，在这里，有回忆。这是一家电影形式的咖啡酒吧，它的门脸虽小，但二楼及露台别有乾坤——老电影海报诉说着那个年代的故事，褪色的胶片电影盒里流淌着岁月的痕迹。来到这儿，你可以留下专属于自己的记忆，告诉心中的那个 TA，我来了，你在哪儿！

16mm is a magic length, and people condense the infinite world into the film which it measures. When unfolding it, we open the memory. At this moment, the memory is open in a bar located at South Luoguxiang Alley, and the eye-catching film logo of the bar tells that there is memory here. This is a film-style coffee bar. The façade of the bar is small, but the 2nd floor and the balcony have a different universe—the posts of the old films recounts the stories of that era and the faded film box flows the imprint of the time. To come here, you may leave your own memory, tell him/her in your heart that I am her, and ask where you are.

地址 (Add)：南锣鼓巷 57 号 /57 Nanluoguxiang Alley
电话 (Tel)：8610-6406 3863
特色 (Themed)：影视主题咖啡馆 /The Film and Television Theme Cafe
地铁 (Subway)：6 号线南锣鼓巷站 A 出口 /Exit A of Nanluoguxiang Station, Line 6

创可贴 T 恤
Plastered T-shirts
中西文化原来可以这样结合
The Chinese and Western Cultures Can Be So Melted

当中国元素像创可贴一样，被一个个贴在T恤衫上的时候，将产生怎样的视觉冲击波？请跟着我，到南锣鼓巷这家叫做"创可贴8"的小店一探究竟。店主是地道的英国人，却起了个地道的中国名——江森海。这个地道的英国人，把地道的中国物件和标语印在了地道的舶来品——T恤衫上，纸质的地铁票，带把儿的大瓷缸子，"1.20元/公里"的出租车计价标准……就这样印在了人们身上，穿行在了北京的大街小巷。

地址 (Add)：南锣鼓巷61号 /61 Nanluoguxiang Alley

电话 (Tel)：8610-6406 4872

特色 (Themed)：创意T恤 /T-shirts With Design of Beijing Color

地铁 (Subway)：6号线南锣鼓巷站 A 出口 /Exit A of Nanluoguxiang Station, Line 6

网址 (Website)：www.plasteredtshirts.com

When the Chinese elements are pasted on the T-shirts like the woundplasts, what kind of visual shockwave will arise? Please follow me to explore the small store so-called Woundplast 8 in the South Luoguxiang Alley. The store keeper is a genuine British, but has a typical Chinese name Jiang Senhai. This genuine British prints on the typical exotic T-shirts such typical Chinese items and slogans as the paper subway tickets, handled jars and Taxi fare rate 1.2yuan/km, and also prints on the people walking on various streets of Beijing.

皇城脚下四合院

紫地客栈
Purple Courtyard
心灵驿站
The Soul Shelter

地址 (Add)：南锣鼓巷沙井胡同甲 24 号 /A 24 Shajing Hutong, Nanluoguxiang Alley

电话 (Tel)：8610-6405 2375

特色 (Themed)：特色客房 /Featured Guestrooms

地铁 (Subway)：6 号线南锣鼓巷站 A 出口 /Exit A of Nanluoguxiang Station, Line 6

　　皇城脚下，紫气东来，属地沙井，是为紫地。在古巷深处，古都中轴线旁，有一个小小的紫地客栈，南望景山公园，北邻钟鼓楼，闹中取静，整洁雅致。如果你玩累了，想找个歇脚的地方，这里是不错的选择。夕阳西下，窝在露台上，任由咖啡的浓香浸润自己，让心情放飞在这诗意的胡同。

By the Imperial City walls, purple nimbus comes from the East, the phenomenon is regarded as propitious omen, and the area is regarded as purple area. With Jingshan Park to its south and the Bell and Drum Tower to its north, the little "Purple Courtyard" stands by the central line of the ancient city. It is neat and snug, peaceful and quiet in noisy surroundings. Whenever you are tired and would seek somewhere to relax, the "Purple Courtyard" would be a wonderful choice. Watching sunset on the balcony, leaving yourself being soaked in the scent of coffee, your heart is set free in this poetic hutong.

文宇奶酪
Wenyu Cheese
霸气的宫廷奶酪
Arrogant Imperial Cheese

皇城的霸气遇上不错的手艺，就诞生了南锣鼓巷这家门脸儿虽小，但绝对有脾气的特色小吃店——文宇奶酪店。它只在早上十点半营业，管他队伍排多长，卖完、齐活、歇业。这里的"奶酪"不像西式奶酪那么味重，它是用鲜奶加白糖再加糯米酒精心烤制而成，香气浓郁，入口嫩滑，味道那叫一个清淡。好这口儿、心里又惦记地道北京风味的人，不妨尝尝排长队的滋味。

That the arrogance of the Imperial City meets good handicrafts results in this unique snack store Wenyu Cheese in the south Luoguxiang Alley. Although it is small, it is absolutely characteristic. It is only open at 10:30 in the morning, and close whenever all the stuff is sold out regardless of how long the queue is. The taste of the cheese here is not as heavy as that of the western cheese. The cheese here is meticulously roasted by using the fresh milk, sugar and the glutinous rice wine, is sweet-smelling, tender and soft, and taste bland. Those who like it and is fond of Beijing flavor might as well try the experience of a long queue.

地址 (Add)：南锣鼓巷 49 号（黑芝麻胡同口）/49 Nanluoguxiang Alley (At the Gate of Heizhima Hutong)
电话 (Tel)：8610-6405 7621
特色 (Themed)：奶酪 /Cheese
地铁 (Subway)：6 号线南锣鼓巷站 A 出口 / Exit A of Nanluoguxiang Station, Line 6

文宇奶酪简介

奶酪是清宫廷奶点之一种，曾是皇家御膳之珍品，只有皇亲贵族独享，之后传入民间，被称为食中精品，是老北京的著名小吃。清代诗人有诗赞曰："闲向街头啖一颐，琼浆满饮润枯喉。觉来下咽如脂滑，寒沁心脾爽似秋。"

文宇奶酪继承了传统制作工艺，采用优质鲜牛奶、白糖、糯米酒经烤制而成。口感细滑，色泽光亮，洁白如脂，风味独特。

皇城脚下四合院

茅盾故居
Former Residence of Mao Dun
与大师在简朴四合院里来个心灵约会
To Have a Spiritual Date With the Master in This Simple and Plain Courtyard

南锣鼓巷，北京的文化符号，胡同深处的人文记忆，留下了多少文人墨客的足迹。巷子中东部的后圆恩寺胡同里，一座有着百年历史的二进四合院，是中国现代著名作家茅盾的故居。茅盾曾于1974-1981年居住于此，茅盾逝世后，人们在前院开设了3个陈列室，展出并陈列其生平、生前实物和图片。想亲眼目睹这位大作家手稿、作品初版本和信件的人，不妨到这里和大师来场心灵约会。

The South Luoguxiang Alley is the cultural symbol of Beijing, and in the people's memory of the deep alley remain many literatus' footprints. In the middle-east part of Houyuan'en Temple Hutong there lies a two-row courtyard with a history of one hundred years, which is the former residence of Mao Dun the contemporary outstanding writer of China. Mao Dun used to live here from 1974 to 1981, and after his death, people set up in the foreyard three exhibition rooms to display and exhibit his life story, his properties and pictures. Those who would like to personally see the master's manuscripts and the original version of works and letters might as well come here to have a spiritual appointment with the master.

地址 (Add)：交道口南大街后圆恩寺胡同 13 号 /13 Houyuan'ensi Hutong, Jiaodaokou South Street
电话 (Tel)：8610-6404 0520
特色 (Themed)：名人故居 /Former Residence of the Celebrity Mao Dun
地铁 (Subway)：6 号线南锣鼓巷站 A 出口 /Exit A of Nanluoguxiang Station, Line 6

古韵坊怡景酒店
MU HOTEL
明清木艺主题酒店
Wood Art Theme Hotel of the Ming and Qing Dynasties

在时尚老街南锣鼓巷星罗棋布的胡同里，有一家明清木艺主题酒店，下榻于此，躺在特制的中式木床上，欣赏着一件件精雕细琢的红木家具，以及点缀其间的青花瓷，一股清雅含蓄、端庄风华的东方气息将扑面而来。这里北临中轴线钟鼓楼，南望故宫天安门，西接后海，东连雍和宫国子监，皇城脚下老北京的古韵之旅，就从这里开始。

In the numerous Hutongs of South Luoguxiang Alley the fashion old street, there is situated a wood art theme hotel of the Ming and Qing Dynasties. Staying in this hotel, lying in the specially made Chinese style bed, and appreciating each piece of red-sandalwood furniture finely made as well as the dotted blue and white porcelain, you will feel an elegant, implicative and dignified oriental flavor blowing against your face. It is close to Zhonggu Tower in the north, adjacent to the Forbidden City and Tiananmen in the south, next to Houhai in the west, and links Lama Temple and the Imperial College in the east. The old flavor trip around old Beijing at the foot of the Imperial City starts from here.

地址 (Add)：交道口南大街菊儿胡同 33 号 /33 ju'er Hutong, Jiaodaokou South Street

电话 (Tel)：8610-8403 2899

特色 (Themed)：中式客房 /Chinese Traditional Guestrooms

地铁 (Subway)：6 号线南锣鼓巷站 A 出口 /Exit A of Nanluoguxiang Station, Line 6

Quadrangle Courtyards by the Imperial City Walls

皇城脚下四合院

古巷贰拾号商务会所
Beijing Guxiang 20 Hotel
商旅度假的世外桃源
Shangri-La for Business, Travel & Vacation

在最富有老北京遗韵的南锣鼓巷，沿着雨蚀风残的青石小路，经过三三两两的颇有胡同趣味的酒吧和个性小店，你会被眼前这座自然古朴的建筑所吸引，红檐碧瓦的木门、惟妙惟肖的石狮、青灰石雕的石墙，让你仿佛回到了旧时的皇家私人宅院，这就是北京古巷贰拾号商务会所。站在会所平台上，鸟瞰古巷四合院的京韵风采，北海的白塔、景山的凉亭、故宫的后檐尽收眼底……

Along the historical bluestone path of Nanluoguxiang Alley, passing by a few Hutong-style bars and novelty shops, you would be attracted by this building with antique simplicity – Beijing Guxiang 20 Hotel. The green tileroof, the red eaves, the carved grey stone walls, and the vivid stone lions, all these bring you back to a royal mansion in ancient time courtyards. Standing on the platform of the club, you will have a bird view of the old style Beijing quadrangle courtyards. The platform also afford a fine view of the White Dagoba in Beihai Park, the pavilion in Jingshan Park, and the back eaves in the Forbidden City.

地址 (Add)：南锣鼓巷 20 号 /20 Nanluoguxiang Alley
电话 (Tel)：8610-6400 5566
特色 (Themed)：特色客房、中国传统美食、吴越楼博物馆 /Featured Guestrooms, Chinese Traditional Cuisine, Wu-Yue Building Museum
地铁 (Subway)：6 号线南锣鼓巷站 A 出口 /Exit A of Nanluoguxiang Station, Line 6

Quadrangle Courtyards by the Imperial City Walls

秦唐府七号院
Courtyard 7
北京首家利用地源热泵技术的四合院酒店
The First Courtyard Hotel in Beijing Using Geothermal Heat Pump System

　　不知是巧合还是有意为之，秦唐府，是用中国历史上最强盛的两个朝代——秦朝和唐朝的名字命名的。三进的院落花木扶疏，木雕、石桌、游廊，让你的心情盛开在这个充满中国情调的院落里。客房里中国味十足的雕花架床、罗汉床，做工考究的实木仿古家具，以及那一束绽放在墙上的画中花儿，让你有了一份梦回秦唐盛世的期待。

Whether it is coincidental or intentional? The Chinese name of the hotel contains the names of two powerful Chinese Dynasties – Qin and Tang. Together with the stone table, woodcarvings, veranda in the yard, and bed with carved patterns, antique reproduction furniture, and the flower blooming in the painting hanging on the wall inside the rooms, the hotel leads you to a dream back to Qin and Tang.

地址 (Add)：南锣鼓巷前鼓楼苑胡同 7 号 /7 Qiangulouyuan Hutong, Nanluoguxiang Alley

电话 (Tel)：8610-6406 0777

特色 (Themed)：四合院特色客房、法式西餐及中式私房菜 /Courtyard Featured Guestrooms, French Cuisine, Chinese Private Home Cuisine

地铁 (Subway)：6 号线南锣鼓巷站 A 出口 / Exit A of Nanluoguxiang Station, Line 6

网址（Website）：www.courtyard7.com

皇城脚下四合院

胡同仁庭院酒店
Hutongren Courtyard Hotel
古典四合院里感受中式茶文化
To Experience the Chinese-style Tea culture in the Classical Courtyard

　　隐匿在小菊儿胡同里的这个四合院,远离繁华和喧嚣,古朴典雅,清新安逸,随处可见的绿色植物,让人有了随时都能亲近大自然的舒畅。免费的茶道课程,让茶道爱好者大呼过瘾。独具特色的客房装修,一草一木、器具摆设都是独具匠心,茶的悠远,四合院的清雅,房间的舒适,别人都来了,你还在等什么?

Hidden in the little Ju'er Hutong, this courtyard is far away from the hustle and bustle, simple and elegant, fresh and comfortable. The green plant everywhere ushers you in a cheerful countenance of being close to the nature any time. The free teaism course really excites the fanciers of the teaism. Distinctive room decoration, every tree and bush, and furnishing and fitting of the utensils show unique ingenuity. Others are coming here to experience the long history of the tea, the elegance of the courtyard, and the comfort of the rooms, and then, what are you waiting for?

地址 (Add):交道口南大街菊儿胡同 71 号 /71 ju'er Hutong, Jiaodaokou South Street
电话 (Tel):8610-8402 4218
特色 (Themed):中式客房、茶艺表演 /Chinese Traditional Guestrooms, Tea Art
地铁 (Subway):6 号线南锣鼓巷站 A 出口 /Exit A of Nanluoguxiang Station, Line 6

得着小馆
Dezhe Restaurant
有着人文气质的川菜馆
A Literary Sichuan Cuisine Restaurant

得着小馆与南锣鼓巷相望于交道口南大街的吉祥胡同里，是名模李艾开的川菜馆。推开厚重的木门，一排书架卷着书香气扑面而来，让小馆立刻有了几分人文气息。青石板的地上铺着大块的波斯风情地毯，中庭的天井上垂着慵懒的吊兰，饕餮之徒们正在厚实的木头桌椅旁埋头苦吃，于是有了撸起袖子大吃一场的冲动。

Across the South Jiaodaokou Street, the restaurant faces Nanluoguxiang Alley in Jixiang Hutong. Famous fashion model Li Ai is the owner of this Sichuan Cuisine Restaurant. Behind the heavy timber door, you will see a shelf of books. A literary atmosphere is thus fostered with the fragrance of the books. The flagstone paved floor is covered with Persian carpet. Spider plants are hanging indolently in the patio. Putting yourself among those gourmands sitting in the heavy wooden chairs, you will feel the impulsion for voracity.

地址 (Add)：交道口南大街北吉祥胡同 1 号 / 1 Beijixiang Hutong, Jiaodaokou South Street
电话 (Tel)：8610-6407 8615
特色 (Themed)：川菜、私房菜 / Sichuan Cuisine, Private Home Cooking
地铁 (Subway)：6 号线南锣鼓巷站 A 出口 / Exit A of Nanluoguxiang Station, Line 6

北锣鼓巷、鼓楼周边
Beiluoguxiang Alley, Gulou and about

鼓楼，古都中轴线的北端起点，为老北京城的报时台。

北锣鼓巷，因多锣鼓之商，又在鼓楼东大街之北，故得名。

穿越南锣鼓巷的灯红酒绿，不知不觉走入了北锣鼓巷的温柔静谧。让我们在暮鼓晨钟中，一起聆听鼓楼周边的老胡同给我们讲从前的故事……

Gulou, or the Drum Tower, being the north end of the ancient city axis, served as the clock for Beijing in the past.

The Beiluoguxiang Alley accommodated many businessmen of the gong and drum and it is to the north of Gulou East Street. That is why it is called "Beiluoguxiang Alley".

Walking through the feasting and revelry of the Nanluoguxiang Alley, people have walked into the serenity and gentleness of the Beiluoguxiang before they knew it. Let us listen to the old stories told by the hutong while enjoying the bell and drum melodies.

34. 如果客栈 Siif Design Hotel / 52
35. 早春二月新川菜 Spring Trees Restaurant / 53
36. 44号猫咪咖啡馆 No.44 Cat Theme Cafe / 54
37. 猫小院主题咖啡西餐厅 Cat Theme Cafe / 55
38. 金色凉山 Golden Liangshan / 56
39. 未名四合院酒店·宝钞店 Weiming Courtyard Hotel · Baochao Branch / 57
40. 吉庆堂宾馆 Ji House / 58
41. 丽江庭院之柔软时光 Lijiang Club of Soft Time / 59
42. 宝月出品 Baoyue Restaurant / 60
43. 东方尚书 Dongfang Shangshu Art &Leisure Courtyard / 61
44. 云洱小镇 Yun'er Town / 62
45. 昔巷怀旧主题餐厅 Haloing the Past Theme Restaurant / 63
46. 合家立四合院 Backhome Courtyard View Hotel / 64

如果客栈
Siif Design Hotel
时尚设计旅店
A Fashionable Hotel

地址 (Add)： 鼓楼东大街北锣鼓巷 57 号 /57 Beiluoguxiang Alley, Gulou East Street

电话 (Tel)： 8610-6406 9496

提示 (Tips)： 所有房间均禁烟。暂时不接受信用卡，房费及押金需于入住时使用现金或借记卡支付。All rooms are no smoking. Pay in cash or debit card, no credit card.

特色 (Themed)： 提供自行车及英文地图。周五、周六有电音派对。There are Electronic Music Parties on Fridays and Saturdays. Bicycles and maps in English are provided.

地铁 (Subway)： 地铁 2 号线北新桥站 D 出口 /Exit D of Beixinqiao Station, Line 2

网址（Website）： www.siif.com

57 号，Siif 设计旅店，宁静而安逸，笑迎京城晨昏。温暖的原木色和明亮的大落地窗，尽情吸纳着每一缕阳光的温柔。中庭生长着两棵北京四合院常见的香椿树，树下有金鱼和睡莲在大瓷缸里悠游自在。我们每天清晨打开店门，等你来；每天夜晚留一盏灯，等你回。如果你没有带着故事来，希望你带着故事走。

Passing through the feast and revelry of Nanluoguxiang Alley, there lies the tender and quiet Beiluoguxiang Alley. Siif is located at No. 57 in the street. The French windows introduce every ray of sunshine into the rooms, two Chinese toon tree grow in the yard, and the goldfishes swim leisurely through water lily in the big jar under the trees. Every morning, the door is open here for your coming; every evening, a light is on for your return. If you bring no story here, we hope you would take story away.

早春二月新川菜
Spring Trees Restaurant
在胡同里邂逅阳光和美食
To Meet the Sunlight and Delicacies in the Hutong

一座古旧的民宅，看似很不起眼，进去后却是别有洞天，优雅干净的大堂，一棵枣树，一棵椿树，和建筑巧妙地设计到了一起。玻璃天窗，任阳光肆意地洒在美食上。和三五好友，品"古法坛子肉"和"两江麻辣鱼"，让你觉得，自己的世界里天天都是早春二月。

An old civil residence seems not very eye-catching, but inside is a different world. The hall is elegant and clean, and a date tree and an Ailanthus tree are ingeniously designed with the architecture. The glass scuttles leads the sunlight willfully shine on the delicacies. To invite a couple of good friends to taste the diced pork in a pot cooked in an ancient way and the peppered and spicy fish from two rivers, you will feel that everyday you are living in the early spring of February.

地址 (Add)：安定门内大街车辇店胡同18号 /8 Cheniandian Hutong, Andingmennei Street
电话 (Tel)：8610-6406 9521
特色 (Themed)：新川菜 /New Sichuan Cuisine
地铁 (Subway)：2号线安定门站A出口 /Exit A of Andingmen Station, Line 2

44号猫咪咖啡馆
No.44 Cat Theme Cafe
让猫咪俘获你流浪的心
To Let the Kitty Capture Your Tramping Heart

这里不盛产猫屎咖啡，这里只盛产爱心，这里是44号猫咪咖啡馆。安定门外的这座四合小院，正如它所处的位置一样让一切都那么安然淡定。店里有20多只猫咪，都是被店主救助的，虽然曾经流浪，却没有任何流浪的窘态，一个个都那么干净、有尊严。来到这里，窝在充满童趣的榻榻米房间和猫咪亲密接触，喝一杯咖啡，尝一口店主亲手制作的甜点，流浪的心顿时找到了归宿。

It does not produce Kopi Luwak coffee here, but produce benevolence. Here is No. 44 Kitty Cafe. Outside Andingmen, this courtyard lets everything calm and reserved just as where it is located. This shop breeds more than 20 cats that are all saved by the Caf owner. Although they used to lead a vagrant life, we can not see any tramping embarrassment, and each of them is so clean and dignified. To come here to nest yourself in the childlike tatami room to closely touch the cats, drink a cup of coffee and taste the sweet personally prepared by the shop owner, you will find the home for your tramping heart.

地址 (Add)：安定门内大街北锣鼓巷44号 /44 Beiluoguxiang Alley, Andingmennei Street

电话 (Tel)：010-6404 0308

特色 (Themed)：咖啡，简餐，萌猫，流浪猫救助 /Cafe, Light Meal, Sprout Cat, Stray Cats Shelter

地铁 (Subway)：2号线安定门地铁站B出口 /Exit B of Andingmen Station, Line 2

猫小院主题咖啡西餐厅
Cat Theme Cafe
爱猫人士的心灵驿站
The Soul Stage of the Cat Fanciers

　　在喧嚣的都市，不只有流浪的猫咪。猫小院，专门收容流浪的心，让繁忙的都市人给自己的心找一个家，让猫友们有一个心灵休憩之所。这里有高大通透的阳光房，有幽静沁凉的水系，有迎风摇曳的紫竹，甚至有和你说话的鸟，屋顶游弋的鱼和一棵漂亮的大树！你可以慵懒地窝在沙发里，和美丽猫咪放松游戏，曼妙的音乐和美酒不知哪个更令人心醉……

In the hustling and bustling capital, there are not only the tramping cats. The cat yard is a special place to house the tramping cats, and let the cat fanciers have a rest place for their souls. In this court, there are big and transparent spacious sunrooms, a shady and cool water system, the purple bamboos waving in the breeze, even the birds that will communicate with you, the fish frolicking on the roof and a large beautiful tree. You may indolently nest yourself in a sofa and play with the cute cats. Whether is the beautiful music or the tasty wine more enchanting?

地址 (Add)：北锣鼓巷北下洼子胡同 14 号 /14 Beixiawazi Hutong, Beiluoguxiang Alley

电话 (Tel)：010-5914 6478

特色 (Themed)：西餐、猫咪 / Western-style Food, Cat

地铁 (Subway)：2 号线安定门地铁站 B 出口 /Exit B of Andingmen Station, Line 2

皇城脚下四合院

金色凉山
Golden Liangshan
胡同里的彝族天堂
The Paradise of Yi Minority in the Hutong

　　北京的金山上光芒照四方，照到了凉山彝族的心坎里，照到了北锣鼓巷幽深的胡同里，照亮了眼前这座二进四合院的金色招牌——金色凉山。金色凉山主营彝族人家私房菜，就餐大厅用墨绿、宝蓝、金黄构成了精美的彩图，与顶部悬挂的白底红花的瓷灯相呼应，中式复古不失时尚典雅，沉稳大气中不乏中国味道，列座其中，或举觞豪饮，壮怀激烈；或品茗倾诉，寄托情怀。了解真正的彝族文化就从这儿开始吧！

The glazing rays on Beijing golden hills shine everywhere, enlightening the heart of the Yi Minority in Liangshan, kindling the deep and serene Hutong in Beiluoguxiang Alley, and illuminating the golden signboard of this two-row courtyard — Golden Liangshan. Golden Liangshan mainly operates the private cuisines of the Yi Minority, and the dining hall applies the colors of deep green, sapphire blue and golden yellow, constituting an exquisite color picture and echoing with the porcelain lamp which is red flowered on the white base and suspends on the top. The Chinese retro style does not lose the elegant fashion, and the calmness and magnificence does not lack the Chinese flavor. Sitting in this restaurant, you may booze and express your bold minds, or sip the tea and confide to attach their feelings. To get to know the Yi Minority's culture starts out from here!

地址 (Add)：北锣鼓巷 91 号 /91Beiluoguxiang Alley

电话 (Tel)：8610-5909 1339

特色 (Themed)：彝族人家私房菜、婚宴 /Yi's Private Home Cuisine, Wedding Banquet

地铁 (Subway)：6 号线南锣鼓巷站 A 出口 /Exit A of Nanluoguxiang Station, Line 6

未名四合院酒店·宝钞店
Weiming Courtyard Hotel · Baochao Branch
精品酒店里的民族乐器馆
The Folk Music Instrument Museum in the Exquisite Hotel

地址 (Add)：宝钞胡同甲 38 号 /A 38 Baochao Hutong
电话 (Tel)：8610-8402 5337
特色 (Themed)：中式客房 /Chinese Guestrooms
地铁 (Subway)：2 号线安定门站 A 出口 /Exit A of Andingmen Station, Line 2

宝钞胡同，元代的"金融街"，财富的聚集地，现如今，这里摇身一变，成了设计师和文人的集结地。一件件被赋予生命和灵性的作品就诞生在这个精神财富的聚集地。未名四合院精品酒店就是其中一件不可多得的生活艺术品。酒店的客房以中国传统民族乐器命名，徜徉其间，仿佛置身在民族乐器博物馆中。

Baochao Hutong used to be the financial street of the Yuan Dynasty and the hub of the wealth, but now it has suddenly been transformed into a staging area for the designers and literatus. One piece of works after another, which is endowed with life and spirit, has been born in this spiritual and wealth hub. Weiming Courtyard exquisite hotel is one of the living arts hard to get, and its guestrooms are named after the Chinese traditional folk music instruments. Wandering in the rooms, you will feel like being in the national musical instrument museum.

Quadrangle Courtyards by the Imperial City Walls

吉庆堂宾馆
Ji House
中国传统文化的乐享地
The Happy-land of the Chinese Traditional Culture

悠悠的庭院，金鱼池，加上古老的柿子树，就是吉庆堂宾馆的写照。来到这里，各种"吉"字组成的图案映入眼帘，"吉祥高照"的寓意让人心情大好，特色的雕饰和彩绘让人很难将这里与现代化的宾馆联系到一起。书法、收藏和太极文化让人眼前一亮，独特的装修风格，简洁却不失高雅，独享闹市中的一隅安静祥和，古筝、咖啡、红酒、象棋，中西文化相融合，古今历史相结合……一切都恰到好处。

The cozy garden, golden fish pond and the old persimmon tree are the real portraiture of Jiqingtang Hotel. To come here, you will find different kinds of Ji character designs heaving in sight. The implied meaning of "Happy and Auspicious" makes people feel good, and characteristic carvings and colorful paintings make it difficult for people to link here with the modernized hotel. Calligraphy, collection and Tai Chi culture let people's eyes brighten. Its unique decoration style is simple and plain, but does not lose elegance, enjoying alone the peace and auspiciousness of the corner in the downtown. Guzheng, coffee, wine and chess combine the Chinese culture with the western culture, and the ancient history with the modern history. Everything is just perfect.

地址（Add）： 北锣鼓巷纱络胡同 7 号 /7 Shaluo Hutong, Beiluoguxiang Alley
电话（Tel）： 8610-8404 3131/6404 3838
特色（Themed）： 中式客房 /Chinese Guestrooms
地铁（Subway）： 2 号线安定门站 A 出口 /Exit A of Andingmen Station, Line 2

丽江庭院之柔软时光
Lijiang Club of Soft Time
云南自助火锅主题餐厅
Yunnan Hotpot Buffet Theme Restaurant

　　国旺胡同，不起眼的小红门，按门铃进去，一个个热气腾腾的小火锅让你浑身立刻充满了暖意，不用点菜，不用动脑子，服务员便按照云南"三叠水宴席"的方式给上三次菜，让你真正享受一回饭来张口的待遇。用餐完毕，找个角落闲坐，任阳光抚摸，忆丽江往事，独享一段柔软时光。

Ring the doorbell of an obscure small red door in the Guowang Hutong and go inside, you will feel warm immediately when seeing steaming little hotpots. Without any order or any brain work by you, the waiter will bring you three dishes according to Yunnan Three-cascade Banquet, and let you really enjoy eating a ready-cooked meal. After the meal, you may find a corner to sit, let the sunshine fondle yourself, recall the past in Lijiang, and enjoy a period of soft time.

地址 (Add)：旧鼓楼大街国旺胡同 18 号 /18 Guowang Hutong, Jiugulou Street

电话 (Tel)：8610-8404 8836

特色 (Themed)：云南小火锅 /Yunnan Hotpot

地铁 (Subway)：2 号线鼓楼大街站 A 2 出口 /Exit A2 of Guloudajie Station, Line 2

皇城脚下四合院

宝月出品
Baoyue Restaurant
胡同私房菜的出品地
Provenance of the Hutong Private Dishes

　　宝月出品开在旧鼓楼大街汤公胡同宝哥和月姐住的老房子里，幽静的胡同，不大的院子，古朴的装修，一如这里出品的私房菜那样平易亲民。宝哥是香港美食协会北京分会主席黄锡源先生的门徒，又跟随世界美食养生协会会长张文彦先生学习管理。不想多花银子又喜好胡同私房菜，一定要来趟宝月出品。纯粹的私家品质，绝对的大众消费。

Baoyue Restaurant is open at the old house of Baoge and Yuejie in the old Gulou Street. The secluded and quiet Hutong, a not big court and the plain decoration are as amicable as the private dishes produced here. Baoge is the disciple of Mr Huang Xiyuan chairman of Hong Kong Food Association Beijing Branch, and goes after Mr Zhang Wenyan Chairman of the World Food and Health Association to learn the management. If you do not want to spend too much money, but like the Hutong private dishes, you should come to Baoyue Restaurant. The purely private quality, but the absolute public consumption.

地址 (Add)：旧鼓楼大街汤公胡同 19 号 /19 Tanggong Hutong, Jiugulou Street

电话 (Tel)：8610-6404 0722

特色 (Themed)：北京菜、私房菜 /Beijing Cuisine, Private Home Cuisine

地铁 (Subway)：2 号线、8 号线鼓楼大街站 G 出口 /Exit G of Guloudajie Station, Line 2 or Line 8

东方尚书
Dongfang Shangshu Art & Leisure Courtyard
文艺小院儿
An Artistic Small Courtyard

古朴的胡同里，优雅的小院，各种各样的盆栽，给人心旷神怡的感觉。这里有大大的阳光棚，舒适的中式沙发，一阵阵龙脑的清香飘来，心情也顿时好了很多。点上喜爱的美食，挑选自己喜欢的书籍，不仅饱了口福，还饱了眼福。没有后海的喧嚣，没有南锣的市井，这里呈现的，是真正的老北京文艺范儿。

In the ancient alley, the elegant courtyard and a variety of plants give people fresh feelings. There are big sun rooms and comfortable Chinese-style sofas. As a burst of borneol fragrance drifts, you will immediately feel a lot better. To order some favorite food and choose some books you like, you can not only eat delicious food, but also comfort your eyes. Without the hustle and bustle of Houhai or the noise of Nanluoguxiang Alley, what presents here is the real old Beijing literary style.

地址 (Add)：安定门内大街北下洼子胡同 12 号 /12 Beixiawazi Hutong, Andingmennei Street

电话 (Tel)：8610-6400 3968

特色 (Themed)：维也纳玫瑰咖啡、自制纸浆泥 /Vienna Rose Coffee, Self-made Paper Clay

地铁 (Subway)：2 号线安定门站 A 出口 /Exit A of Andingmen Station, Line 2

皇城脚下四合院

云洱小镇
Yun'er Town
微缩版的云南古镇餐厅
A Miniature Version of Yunnan Old Town Restaurant

"滇香引出世中仙，鲜味勾来云外客"，彩云之南的珍馐美味落户北京胡同，让好吃客们在皇城脚下，亦能做一回世中仙、云中客。汽锅鸡、野生菌、香茅草烤鱼……一桌美味在蜡染的桌布上魅力四射，让你的心也随着摇曳的红灯笼荡漾起来。微缩版的云南古镇等你来。

"Yunnan's fragrance attracts the fairy of the world, and the delicious taste allures the guest afar from the clouds". The delicious food from the south of the colorful clouds settles in the Hutong of Beijing will give the fancy diners, at the foot of the Imperial City, the chance to become the fairy of the world and the guest afar from the clouds. A table of delicacies such as the steam-boiled chicken, wild fungus and lemon grass fish glamour on the batik table-cloth, and let your heart flicker with the bobbling red lanterns. A miniature version of the ancient town of Yunnan waits for you to come.

地址 (Add)：北锣鼓巷 84 号 /84 Beiluoguxiang Alley
电话 (Tel)：8610-8404 2407
特色 (Themed)：云南菜馆 /Yunnan Cuisine
地铁 (Subway)：6 号线南锣鼓巷站 A 出口 /Exit A of Nanluoguxiang Station, Line 6

昔巷怀旧主题餐厅
Haloing the Past Theme Restaurant
给祖国花朵的童年回忆
To Give the Flowers of the Motherland the Childhood Memory

准备好了吗，时刻准备着，我们都是曾被称为祖国花朵的一代人，一群永远长不大的孩子和一群忘记了自己曾经是孩子的大人们！红领巾、三道杠、红蓝铅笔、红花榜，昔巷的一切，把我们拉回到了那期待着放学、期待着游戏的童年。麦乳精、杂粮饭……这里将把最黄金的体魄贡献给"祖国的花朵"们。

Are you ready? We are prepared for any time. We were once known as the generation of the flowers of the motherland, a group of children who have never grown up and a group of adult who have forgotten that they used to be the children! Everything in Xixiang such as the red scarf, three bars, blue and red pencils, red flower lists and so on, brings us back to the childhood during which we were waiting for class dismissal and games. Malt, grains of rice... The restaurant here will contribute the best physique to "the flowers of our motherland".

地址 (Add)：鼓楼东大街大经厂西巷 3 号 /3 Dajingchangxixiang, Gulou East Street

电话 (Tel)：8610-6406 5852

特色 (Themed)：家常菜、私房创意菜 /Private Home Cuisine

地铁 (Subway)：6 号线南锣鼓巷站 A 出口 /Exit A of Nanluoguxiang Station, Line 6

皇城脚下四合院

合家立四合院
Backhome Courtyard View Hotel
和热情的街坊邻居侃北京
To Talk About Beijing With the Warm-hearted Neighbors

一个90后，一个靠双脚走天下的"老"驴子，最终选择在传统与现代人文完美融合的奇幻城市——北京，创立一家属于自己、属于大家，四海之内合家欢乐的四合院旅馆。古典的架子床和老式的太师椅，四星级的客房，五星级的床，还可以DIY早餐。寻求美食的人，来吧，簋街、南锣鼓巷、鼓楼、后海，走路10分钟任你吃个够；寻找老北京文化的人，来吧，这儿有最热情的街坊邻居跟你侃北京！

An "old" donkey, born after 1990 and travelling around on his own feet, eventually chooses Beijing a fantasy city where the tradition and the modern humanity are perfectly integrated, and inaugurates a cheerful courtyard hotel which belongs to himself and anyone, and welcome everyone from all over the world. The hotel is equipped with the classical shelf bed and old armchair, four-star rooms and five-star beds, and you can also DIY your breakfast. This is a good place for those who search for delicacy. It takes about 10 minutes by walk from the hotel, you can eat a lot in such places as Guijie street, Nanluoguxiang Alley, Gulou, and Houhai. Please come, those who search for the old Beijing culture. The warm-hearted neighbors there will talk about Beijing with you.

地址 (Add)：西公街1号 /1 Xigong Street
电话 (Tel)：8610-6405 0827
特色 (Themed)：老北京风格中式客房 /Traditional Beijing Style Guestrooms
地铁 (Subway)：5号线北新桥站A出口 /Exit A of Beixinqiao Station, Line 5

雍和宫、五道营周边
Lama Temple, Wudaoying and About

雍和宫位于北京市东城区内城的东北角即雍和宫大街路东，是北京市内最大的藏传佛教寺院。康熙的四皇子也就是以后的雍正皇帝曾在这里住过，雍正驾崩后，乾隆帝把雍和宫改建成了藏传喇嘛寺庙。

与雍和宫一街之隔的是五道营民俗文化休闲胡同，这里因明朝时驻扎过军队而得名。胡同南边就是中国历史文化名街——国子监街，见证着老街荣耀与繁华的孔庙就伫立一旁。

如果你厌倦了南锣鼓巷的喧嚣，不妨到这里来个国学启蒙和宗教文化之旅。

地铁2号线、5号线"雍和宫"站出来即到。

The Lama Temple is located in the northeast of the Dongcheng District, or east to the Lama Temple Street. The temple is the largest Tibetan Buddhism temple in the city. Yongzheng, the fourth son of the Emperor Kangxi, once lived here. After Yongzheng passed away, the successor, Emperor Qianlong reconstructed the Yonghe Palace into the Tibetan Buddhist Lama Temple.

To the other side of the Lama Temple Street is Wudaoying Folk Cultural Hutong. In the Ming Dynasty, the battalion was once stationed here and that is why it got the name of Wudaoying(Five Battalion). To the south of the hutong is the famous historical street called Guozijian(the Imperial College), with the Confucian Temple witnessing the glory and prosperity of the old street.

If you are tired of the noise of Nanluoguxiang Alley, why not take a trip to feel the national enlightenment and religious culture?

Take Subway Line 2 or 5 to "Lama Temple" Station and you could find them easily.

47. 乙十六·地坛中心店 Noble Club-16 / 68
48. 京兆尹 Kingsjoy / 69
49. NATOOKE(死飞) / 70
50. CHANGE 交换商店 / 71
51. 润琦缘茶馆（汉宫阙茶餐厅）Hangongque Tea Cafe / 72
52. 朋坐西厨堂 Argo / 73
53. 如是山房 Rushi Shanfang / 74
54. 红云阁龙腾酒店 Grand Hotel Du Palais Rouge / 75
55. 五十六号院私房菜 No. 56 Courtyard / 76
56. 惠量小院 Huiliang Yard / 77
57. 葡萄院儿比萨饼店 Vineyard Cafe / 78
58. 藏红花西餐厅 Saffron Restaurant / 79
59. 印格时光 Life is Elsewhere / 80
60. 泥庐餐厅 Impasto Pizza / 81
61. 钓鱼台雍和酒店 The Diaoyutai Beijing Lama Temple / 82
62. 猜火车电影餐厅 Trainspotting Restaurant / 83
63. 埃蒙小镇 Aimo Town / 84
64. 圣唐古驿文化创意园 Shengtang Guyi Cultural Creativity Park / 85
65. 炮局工厂青年旅舍 P.LOFT Youth Hostel / 86

乙十六·地坛中心店
Noble Club-16
在皇家别院里抚今追昔
To Contemplate the Present and Recall the Past with Emotion in the Imperial Court

  乙十六，地坛公园旁，皇家别院里的高档餐饮品牌，一个用"美食、美景、美物"征服人们味觉、视觉、触觉，把街道门牌号打造成餐饮文化符号的地方。来这里，尝美食，赏美景，凭栏远眺，遥想皇帝当年，地坛祭地后，来此别院小憩，在琼楼玉宇间，品茶纳凉；现如今，小桥流水，转朱阁，低绮户，照着贪恋美景、美食、美器的忘归人，弹指一挥间，岁月沧桑了你我，不变的，是那深深庭院里的古木，还有那一汪池水。

Noble Club-16 near the Ditan Park is a luxury catering brand in the imperial court, and a place using delicious food, beautiful scenery and fine things to conquer people's senses of taste, vision and touch and to transform the street house number into a catering culture symbol. Come here to taste the delicacies, enjoy the scenery, and lean upon balustrade looking into the distance, thinking back those years the emperor came to this unique court to take a short break after offering sacrifice to the earth and sip the tea and relax in the shade among those magnificent palace buildings. But now, the water is flowing beneath the little bridges, and the moon is rounding the exquisite pavilions and doors and windows with carved designs, and lighting upon the person who forgets to go back home because of clinging to the scenery, delicacies and pretty items. With a mere snap of the fingers, the time has changed you and me, but what have not been changed are the old trees in the deep garden and a pond of water.

地址 (Add)：和平里中街乙 16 号 /B16 Hepingli Middle Street
电话 (Tel)：8610-6428 1188
特色 (Themed)：官府菜、淮扬菜 /Royle Cuisine, Huaiyang Cuisine
地铁 (Subway)：5 号线和平里北街站 C 出口 /Exit C of Hepingli North Street Station, Line 5

京兆尹
Kingsjoy
在大爱之所品无味之味
To Taste the Tasteless in the Place of Great Love

无味之味，乃自然之味，乃天人合一之味，此味只应天上有，人间能有几回尝！所幸之事，在京城，在红墙金顶的雍和宫脚下，就有这样一处大爱之所，这里汇集了世界各地原生态植物系食材，用爱，料理，烹制出一道道至味素食。瓦当窗花，竹影扶疏，慢食，乐和，无量仁慈，不负它这么多年来耳濡目染皇家佛寺大慈大爱之名。这里，就是京兆尹。

The taste of the tasteless is the taste of the nature and also the flavor of harmony between the heaven and human. Such a flavor should only exist in the heaven, while there are few chances to taste on the earth! Fortunately, at the foot of Lama Temple with red-walls and golden roofs in the capital of Beijing, there is such a place of great love, where the natural plant food materials all over the world converge, and courses of marvelous vegetarian dishes are cooked out with love and food material ingredients. Eaves tile window flowers, luxuriant and well-spaced bamboo trees, slow eating and joyful music as well as boundless kindness do not let down its fame for being influenced by the great love of the royal buddhist temple for so many years. Here is Kingsjoy Restaurant.

地址 (Add)：五道营胡同 2 号 /2 Wudaoying Hutong
电话 (Tel)：8610-8404 9191
特色 (Themed)：无国界蔬食料理 /Fusion Cuisine
地铁 (Subway)：2 号线、5 号线雍和宫站 D 出口 /Exit D of Lama Temple Station, Line 2 or 5
网址（Website）：www.kingsjoy.com

皇城脚下四合院

NATOOKE（死飞）
固定齿轮自行车店和杂耍用品店
The Fixed-Gear Bicycle Shop and Juggling Article Shop

死飞，一个让年轻人血脉贲张的字眼儿，一个成就了耍酷一族用自行车演绎乐活人生的时尚潮流集散地。你绝想不到的是，店老板伊泉竟是个金发碧眼的女孩儿，来自德国，是北京"死飞"运动的发起人，也是这项运动的专业级高手。想和死党们一起玩到high吗？想用自己的双手DIY自己的最爱吗？来吧，在这青砖灰瓦的胡同里，让那颗不安分的心跳动起来吧！

Natooke is an agonistic word to young men, and a fashion distribution center which help the Mallrats deduce the LOHAS lives by bicycle. What you can not think of is that the shop owner Yi Quan is a blonde girl from Germany, who is the founder of "Natooke" movement in Beijing, and is also the professional ace of this sport. Do you want to be high with these hardcores? And do you want to use your own hands DIY your most loved? Please come here, and in this grey bricks and gray tiles Hutong, beat up your restless heart.

地址 (Add)：五道营胡同甲 19-1 号 /A 19-1Wudaoying Hutong
电话 (Tel)：8610-8402 6925
特色 (Themed)：固定齿轮自行车、杂耍用品 /Fixed Gear Bikes, Juggling Equipment
地铁 (Subway)：2号线、5号线雍和宫站 D 出口 /Exit D of Lama Temple Station, Line 2 or 5

CHANGE 交换商店
北京第一家以物易物的交换商店
The First Barter Exchange Store in Beijing

以物易物，这种最原始的市场行为，如今却卷土重来，成为了一种时尚潮流。如果你够潮，就带着自己用不着的物件来这里吧，兴许，你众里寻它千百度的那个物件，就躲在这里的某个角落，等你带它回家。亮出你的态度，告诉大家，我来啦，我是绿色时尚乐活一族。

Barter used to be the most primary market activity, but now it resurges and becomes a fashion. If you are fashionable enough, you may bring all the stuff out of use and come here. Maybe the article you have been looking for all the time hides somewhere in this store and waits for you to take back home. Show your attitude and tell everyone that I am here and am one of the green fashion LOHAS family.

地址 (Add)：安定门东大街五道营胡同 67 号 /67 Wudaoying Hutong, Andingmen East Street
电话 (Tel)：8610-6407 6094
特色 (Themed)：以物易物 /One Can Exchange Articles Out of Use
地铁 (Subway)：5 号线雍和宫站 D 出口 /Exit D of Lama Temple Station, Line 5
2 号线安定门站 B 出口 /Exit B of Andingmen Station, Line 2

皇城脚下四合院

润琦缘茶馆（汉宫阙茶餐厅）
Hangongque Tea Cafe
汉代宫廷美食文化与中国茶文化的传播者
The Propagator of the Han Dynasty's Palace Food Culture and the Chinese Tea Culture

穿汉服，行汉礼，赏汉乐，品汉食……你可不要认为这是在演古装戏，这可是五道营胡同汉宫阙茶餐厅推出的一道令老外痴迷无比的文化大餐。汉水大煮鹿腿、昭帝钓龙、苏武羊扒、仲景养生粥、御茶水晶虾……单看这些菜名，就已经让人心向往之了。心动不如行动，马上出发，穿越时空，重回汉朝，来一次皇家饮食文化的奇妙之旅吧。

Wear clothes of the Han Dynasty, perform the etiquette of the Han Dynasty, enjoy the music of the Han Dynasty, and eat the food of the Han Dynasty, etc. You should not regard that this is on an ancient costume drama, but this is a grand culture feast which is launched by Hangongque Tea Cafe in Wudaoying Hutong and makes the foreigners really obsessed. Han Water Boiled Deer Leg, Emperor Zhao Catching the Dragon, Su Wu Grilled Lamb Chop, Zhongjing Healthy Porridge, Crystal Shrimp in Royal Tea, etc. Solely look at the names of the dishes, you should already be interested in. Excitement is never better than action. Let's start out now immediately, go through the time tunnel and back to the Han Dynasty, and begin a wonder trip of royal diet culture.

地址 (Add)：五道营胡同 65 号 /65 Wudaoying Hutong
电话 (Tel)：8610-6400 9326
特色 (Themed)：穿汉服，行汉礼，赏汉乐，品汉食 / Wear Clothes of the Han Dynasty, Perform the Etiquette of the Han Dynasty, Enjoy the Music of the Han Dynasty, and Eat the Food of the Han Dynasty
地铁 (Subway)：5 号线雍和宫站 D 出口 /Exit D of Lama Temple Station, Line 5
2 号线安定门站 B 出口 /Exit B of Andingmen Station, Line 2

朋坐西厨堂
Argo
当爱琴海文明遇上老北京四合院
When the Aegean Sea Civilization Meets the Old Beijing Courtyard

朱漆的大门，雪白的墙，爱琴海的文明，老北京的情……当四合院儿遇上希腊菜，除了互相说句"你是我的菜"外，没有再合适的语言来形容开放的北京带给海归和老外们的喜悦了。在包容的环境里，一个希腊人，就这样开始了他在北京、在胡同、在四合院里的喜悦人生。想要品尝正宗希腊菜的朋友，就来朋坐西厨堂吧。

Red lacquer door, white wall, the Aegean Sea civilization, and the old Beijing love, etc. When the courtyard meets the Greek food, other than the language to each other saying "you're my food", there are no other appropriate words to describe the joy the open Beijing brings to the overseas Chinese and foreigners. In a tolerant environment, a Greek so starts his joyful life in Beijing, in the hutong, and in the courtyard. Anyone who wants to taste the authentic Greek food should come to Argo.

地址 (Add)：五道营胡同 59 号 /59 Wudaoying Hutong
电话 (Tel)：8610-8403 9748
特色 (Themed)：希腊地中海菜系 /Greek Mediterranean Cuisine
地铁 (Subway)：5 号线雍和宫站 D 出口 /Exit D of Lama Temple Station, Line 5
　　　　　　　2 号线安定门站 B 出口 /Exit B of Andingmen Station, Line 2

皇城脚下四合院

如是山房
Rushi Shanfang
琴、禅、茶文化主题空间
Qin, Zen and Tea Culture Theme Space

　　山房：山中草房，门掩白墙，茶映疏竹，香绕书影，琴入禅境。如是：或颦或笑，尽是真理的流露；亦琴亦茶，皆为还乡的坦途。当下体认，当下承当，举手投足，无不是道。想要在钢筋水泥的山林中寻得一方心灵隐修处，不妨到与国子监、雍和宫为邻的如是山房，抚琴、品茶、参禅。

Shanfang: The door of the mountain cottage is closed in the white wall, the tea mirrors the sparse bamboos, the incense swirls around the book, and the sound of Qin goes into the conception of zen. Rushi: to frown or smile, all is the expression of the true feelings; and to play the Qin or sip the tea, all is the easy path to return home. Cherish what you have now and keep to what you believe in. All behavior is Tao. If you want to find a quiet place for your heart in the reinforced concrete forest, you might as well call on Rushi Shanfang adjacent to Lama Temple and the Imperial College to play the Qin, sip the tea and practice meditation.

地址 (Add)：五道营胡同 58 号 /58 Wudaoying Hutong

电话 (Tel)：8610-6402 5766

特色 (Themed)：古琴课、茶课、国画课 /Classes about Guqin, Tea and Traditional Chinese Painting

地铁 (Subway)：2 号线、5 号线雍和宫站 A 出口 /Exit A of Lama Temple Station, Line 2 or 5

网址 (Website)：www.Rushishanfang.com

红云阁龙腾酒店
Grand Hotel Du Palais Rouge
龙文化主题酒店
The Dragon Culture Theme Hotel

地址 (Add)： 五道营胡同 57 号 /57 Wudaoying Hutong
电话 (Tel)： 8610-6405 6119
特色 (Themed)： 龙文化主题酒店 /The Dragon Culture Theme Hotel
地铁 (Subway)： 2 号线、5 号线雍和宫站 A 出口 /Exit A of Lama Temple Station, Line 2 or 5

　　在五道营胡同里尝遍美食、尽览各国风情后,到哪儿去歇个脚、打个盹儿,养精蓄锐呢?红云阁龙腾酒店是你的不二选择!这是一家将中国红运用到极致的酒店,在热情似火的中国红里,栩栩如生的金龙盘踞各处,在状似鸟笼的灯笼映照下活灵活现。在这里睡到自然醒,然后开始第二天的雍和宫、国子监、孔庙的国学启蒙之旅,你一定不虚此行!

Where can you go to take a break and have a nap to recuperate your energy after tasting delicacies around and fully enjoying the national customs in Wudaoying Hutong? Grand Hotel Du Palais Rouge is your best choice! This is a hotel which applies the Chinese red to the acme, where the vivid golden dragon in the fiery Chinese red entrenches everywhere and vigorously turns out under the light of birdcage-like lanterns. To wake up naturally from sleep here, and then begin the ancient Chinese literature enlightenment tour the following day to Lama Temple, Confucian Temple and the Imperial College, you surely will not make this tour in vain.

皇城脚下四合院

五十六号院私房菜
No. 56 Courtyard
低调的皇家私房菜馆
The Low-key Royal Private Dish Restaurant

在这个广而告之的时代，把门牌号用作店名的，一定是低调而神秘、有两下子的主儿。这不，推开五道营胡同56号院的朱漆大门，别有洞天在里头。青砖灰瓦，画栋雕梁，青松绿竹，游鱼鹦鹉……你还没回过神儿，店主已然将一把折扇递了上来，上用蝇头小楷工整地书写着菜谱——一个馒头、一个萝卜……这是什么招牌菜？要想知道答案，你呐，得亲自上门，别忘了提前预约。

In the advertising age, the owner of the restaurant who uses the house number as his restaurant's name must be the low-key and mysterious person, and is really something. Well, when you push it open the red-varnished door of No.56 courtyard at Wudaoying Hutong, you will find a hidden but beautiful spot in it such as grey bricks and gray tiles, carved beams and painted rafters, green pines and bamboos, swimming fish and parrot, etc. While you haven't gotten back your composure, the owner hand you a folding fan on which the recipes are neatly written in a very small characters — a steamed bun, a radish, etc. What kind of specialty is it? If you want to know the answer, you have to call the door personally and don't forget to make an appointment in advance.

地址 (Add)：五道营胡同56号 /56 Wudaoying Hutong
电话 (Tel)：8610-6400 3337
特色 (Themed)：私房菜、宫廷菜 /Private Home Cuisine, Royal Cuisine
地铁 (Subway)：2号线、5号线雍和宫站D出口 /Exit D of Lama Temple Station, Line 2 or 5

惠量小院
Huiliang Yard
中国的小院 惠量的心
The Small Chinese Yard Has a Capacious Heart

雍和宫的阳光，安定门的月光，交汇在国子监的金顶上，让绿色的惠量小院，苏醒在每天的午后。品茶，焚香，插花，抚琴，清谈，把玩……听鸟语，闻花香，分享、体验、实践中国式生活。在小院屋顶，看风云，笑风月，听细水潺潺，品茶汤淡淡，思绪，慢慢，漫漫……惠量小院，院小量惠，一个有内容、有高度的地方。

Lama Temple's sunshine and Andingmen's moonlight converge at the golden roof of the Imperial College, and let the green Huiliang Yard revive in the afternoon everyday. You may sip tea, burn incense, arrange flowers, play the Qin, talk freely, appreciate the antique, and so on, and to listen to the birds and smell the flowers to enjoy, experience and practice the Chinese-style life. At the roof of the yard, you may observe the wind and the clouds, laugh at the wind and the moon, listen to the water babbling, sip the tea leisurely, and think slowly and indulgently, etc. Huiliang Yard is small, but it is capacious, and is a place which has content and highness.

地址 (Add)：五道营胡同 35 号 /35 Wudaoying Hutong

电话 (Tel)：8610-13301010105

特色 (Themed)：每周 20 场各类传统活动 / 20 Various Traditional Activities Each Week

地铁 (Subway)：2 号线、5 号线雍和宫站 D 出口 /Exit D of Lama Temple Station, Line 2 or 5

Quadrangle Courtyards by the Imperial City Walls

葡萄院儿比萨饼店
Vineyard Cafe
英伦风情的北京情节
Love in Beijing with British-style

地址 (Add)：五道营胡同 31 号 /31 Wudaoying Hutong
电话 (Tel)：8610-6402 7961
特色 (Themed)：地中海比萨、土豆皮、葡萄酒 /Mediterranean Pizza, Potato Skin, Wine
地铁 (Subway)：2 号线、5 号线雍和宫站 D 出口 /Exit D of Lama Temple Station, Line 2 or 5

雍和宫脚下，五道营胡同，欧式比萨因一个英国小伙儿和一个中国姑娘的结合而绽放出了别样风情。坐在青砖铺就、灰墙覆顶的小院里，阳光从玻璃顶倾泻下来，如沐地中海阳光，欧式家庭菜还有逢客必点的地中海比萨、土豆皮，配上上好的葡萄酒，小桌小椅大比萨，菜鲜唯美小情调，你还不来吗？

At the foot of Lama Temple in Wudaoying Hutong, the European pizza bursts out the unique love when a British guy marries a Chinese girl. Sitting in the court paved with the grey brick and topped with the gray wall, as the sunshine pours down from the glass top, you will feel like bathing in the Mediterranean sun. There are European family food, and the Mediterranean pizza and potato skins every customer will order, plus a bottle of good wine, small tables and chairs and big pizzas. The vegetables are fresh and delicious, and the sentiment is affectionate. Won't you come?

藏红花西餐厅
Saffron Restaurant
地中海风情等你来解
To Understand the Mediterranean Love

小小的五道营胡同就是一个迷你的联合国。离爱琴海文明不远，是地中海风情。藏红花，一家主打西班牙海鲜饭和自制西班牙水果酒的西餐厅，店门外爬满了绿色的爬山虎，让你没进店门，就嗅到了地中海的气息。新鲜的食材，高品质的橄榄油，没有任何添加剂，在这样一间超有爱的餐厅里用餐，谁能不解风情？

The small Wudaoying Hutong is just a mini United Nations. Not far from the Aegean Sea civilization is a Mediterranean style. Saffron Restaurant is a western food restaurant which mainly operates Spanish sea-food meals and homemade Spanish fruit wine. Outside the restaurant climbs the green creepers everywhere, letting you smell the scent of the Mediterranean even without going inside. Fresh food ingredients and high-quality olive oil do not have any additives. Eating in such a super love restaurant, who can not understand love?

地址（Add）：五道营胡同 64 号院 /64 Wudaoying Hutong

电话（Tel）：8610-8404 4909

特色（Themed）：西班牙菜、自制西班牙水果酒 /Spanish Cuisine, Homemade Spanish Fruit Wine

地铁（Subway）：2 号线、5 号线雍和宫站 D 出口 /Exit D of Lama Temple Station, Line 2 or 5

网址（Website）：www.ilovesaffron.com

皇城脚下四合院

印格时光
Life is Elsewhere
西藏记忆的复制地
A Place to Reproduce the Memory of Tibet

地址 (Add)：五道营胡同 18 号 /18 Wudaoying Hutong
电话 (Tel)：8610-6402 1646
特色 (Themed)：西藏风情，咖啡，书 /Tibetan Customs, Coffee, Book
地铁 (Subway)：2 号线、5 号线雍和宫站 D 出口 /Exit D of Lama Temple Station, Line 2 or 5

　　时光不能倒流，但时光里那些关于西藏关于旅行的美好瞬间，却记录在了印格时光里。一家小小的咖啡店，用一个小小的角落复制了印象西藏……舞动的经幡，吉祥的胜利幢，多彩的照片，点缀了小店，也点亮了记忆。燃一支藏香，饮一口酥油茶，读一首仓央嘉措的诗，在雍和宫若隐若现的诵经声里，思绪又飞到了高原上那些明媚的时光里。

You can never turn the clock back, but the beautiful moments of the time about Tibet and about travel are recorded in the shop "Life is Elsewhere". A small Coffee shop uses a small corner to reproduce the impression of Tibet. The dancing prayer flags, auspicious DHVAJA and colorful pictures embellish the small shop and also light up the memory. To burn an incense, drink the buttered tea, and read a poem of Tsangyang Gyatso, you may fly, in the indistinct scripture chanting in Lama Temple, your thoughts back the beautiful days on the plateau.

泥庐餐厅
Impasto Pizza
在时尚典雅中感受奢华美食
To Try the Sumptuous Delicacies in the Fashion and Elegance

地址 (Add)：国子监街 40 号 /40 Guozijian Street
电话 (Tel)：8610-6401 8779
特色 (Themed)：果木比萨、炭烤挪威鳕鱼 /Fruitwood Pizza, Grilled Norway Cod
地铁 (Subway)：2 号线安定门站 B 出口 /Exit B of Andingmen Station, Line 2
网址 (Website)：www.bjcsxs.com.cn

雍和宫金顶红墙折射的霞光映衬着国子监老街，点缀在古柏与蜿蜒胡同中的孔庙见证着这条老街的荣耀与繁华。沿着树影向西，泥庐餐厅掩映其间。身处泥庐，时间仿佛是静止的，处处都是泥土草秸天成的乡野间朴拙有致的风景。通红的泥炉将各种原料汇集腹中，再将芝士的浓香、果木的薰香、原料的鲜香、香草的芳香，融合成纯正的比萨，让你在纯粹的自然之美中开始一段奇妙的美食之旅。

The glow of the sunset refracted by the golden roof and red walls of Lama Temple rays against the old Guozijian Street, and Confucian Temple adorned among the old cypresses and in the zigzag alley witnesses the glory and prosperity of this old street. Along the shade of the trees to the west, you will find Impasto Pizza hidden among the trees. In Impasto Pizza, time seems to be still, and everywhere is the natural mud and grass countryside plain scenery. The glowing mud furnace stuffs with various raw materials, and then mixes together the cheese flavor, fruit wood fragrance, raw material freshness, and smell of vanilla to make the pure pizza, leading you to start a wonderful gourmet journey in pure natural beauty.

皇城脚下四合院

钓鱼台雍和酒店
The Diaoyutai Beijing Lama Temple
二环里的世外桃源
Shangri-La Inside the Second Ring Road in Beijing

霞光映照的历史文化名街国子监街，正在上演着一出视觉与文化大戏。中国唯一的国家级油画专业美术馆——大都美术馆将与雍和精品酒店、温泉 SPA 中心于 2014 年点亮古柏参天的国子监街。仿古四合院，正在缔造着充满东方韵味的简洁之美。从 3000 多米的地下掘取的天然温泉水，必将成就北京二环内独一无二的身心栖息地。

Guozijian was the Chinese name of the Imperial College in the Qing Dynasty. The Street where the College was located thus has the name – Guozijian Street. Here in the street, the only national-level gallery for oil paintings – Dadu Gallery, together with the Diaoyutai Beijing Lama Temple and SPA Center will lighten the winter of 2014. The hotel is antique quadrangle style. With thermal spring dug out of more than 3000 meters deep in the earth, the hotel would be a unique resort inside the second ring road in Beijing.

地址 (Add)：国子监街乙 28 号院
　　　　　 B 28 Guozijian Street
提示 (Tips)：2014 年 10 月开业
　　　　　 Open in October, 2014
地铁 (Subway)：5 号线雍和宫站
　　　　　 D 出口 /Exit D of Lama Temple Station, Line 5

猜火车电影餐厅
Trainspotting Restaurant
中国民间独立电影放映与酒吧放映的先行者
A Pioneer of the Chinese Folk Independent Film Screening and Bar Screening

我们将镜头拉到方家胡同——北京工业史上重要的"机床胡同"。远远地，一列火车驶来，穿过皇城里的"迷你798"，驶向胡同尽头的"LOFT"，悬浮于草坪上。白色的火车车厢上赫然写着"猜火车电影餐厅"几个字。乘客们手里握着"高速行驶，缓慢生活"的车票，开始了一段奇妙的文化与美食之旅。白盒子里的人，沉浸在私人影像表达的世界中；白盒子外的人，沉浸在将老厂房与新建筑完美合成的对话景观中。历史就这样照进了现实。

Let's focus our lens on Fangjia Hutong — the important Machine Tool Hutong in the industrial history of Beijing. From far away, you can see a train approaching, going through the "mini 798" in the Imperial City and to the "LOFT" at the end of the hutong, and suspending on the lawn. On the white train carriage impressively writes a few words "Trainspotting Restaurant". Passengers holding the ticket of "high speed, slow life" begin a fantastic culture and fine food trip. People in the white box are immersed in a world expressed by the private images; while people outside the white box are immersed in the view of the dialogue between the old buildings and new buildings that are perfectly synthesized. The history is so shining into the reality.

地址 (Add)：安定门内大街方家胡同 46 号 / 46 Fangjia Hutong, Andingmennei Street

电话 (Tel)：8610-6406 0658

特色 (Themed)：云南菜、贵州菜、电影 / Yunnan Cuisine, Guizhou Cuisine, Film

地铁 (Subway)：2 号线安定门站 B 出口 / Exit B of Andingmen Station, Line 2

网址 (Website)：www.caihuoche.com.cn

皇城脚下四合院

埃蒙小镇
Aimo Town
在"机床胡同"体验佤族风情
To Experience the Ethnic Custom of the Wa Minority in the Machine Tool Hutong

"机床胡同"不仅有铁骨，亦有柔情，云南原生态的民族文化风情就在胡同里的埃蒙小镇落户。镇长是佤族原创歌手艾芒，一个户外运动爱好者，这里因此也成了户外运动爱好者的聚集地。如果你喜欢云南菜，对原生态的民族文化和户外文化感兴趣，埃蒙小镇不容错过。

"Machine Tool Hutong" has not only the muscles of iron, but also the tender feelings. Yunnan original ecological folk cultural custom is settled at Aimo Town in this hutong. The mayor Aimang is a Wa Minority singer of the original works and therefore this place has been the distribution center for outdoor sports enthusiasts. If you like Yunnan dishes and are interested in the original ecological national culture and the outdoor culture, Aimo Town shall not be missed.

地址 (Add)：安定门内大街方家胡同 46 号 /46 Fangjia Hutong, Andingmennei Street
电话 (Tel)：8610-6400 1725
特色 (Themed)：云南菜系 /Yunnan Cuisine
地铁 (Subway)：2 号线安定门站 B 出口 /Exit B of Andingmen Station, Line 2

Quadrangle Courtyards by the Imperial City Walls

圣唐古驿文化创意园
Shengtang Guyi Cultural Creativity Park
藏经馆胡同里的造梦空间
The Dream-making Space in Cangjingguan Hutong

圣唐古驿文化创意园，西临藏传佛教名刹——雍和宫，南依八百年禅宗伽蓝——柏林寺，38个具有浓郁老北京风情的四合院星罗棋布拱卫于周边。这里不仅是渗透着历史印记与文化传承的圣地，更是创意梦工厂聚集的热土。无论是家具艺术展示，还是高端文化餐饮场所，经造梦空间的打造，都在简约中渗透着东方意向之美，张扬中绽放出时尚气息。

Shengtang Guyi Cultural Creativity Park is close to the renowned Tibetan buddhist temple — Lama Temple in the west, adjacent to the 800-year old Zen Garan — Berlin Temple, and is surrounded by 38 scattered courtyards with rich flavor of old Beijing. Here is not only the holy land permeated with the historic marks and cultural heritage, but also a hot-land for creative dream works to gather together. Whether it is a furniture art exhibition, or a high-grade cultural catering place, they permeate the oriental intention beauty out of simplicity and burst fashion out of flaunting.

地址 (Add)：雍和宫藏经馆胡同2号院 /2 Cangjingguan Hutong, the Lama Temple
电话 (Tel)：8610-5100 6300-100
特色 (Themed)：设计中心、文化艺术中心 /Design Center, Cultural Art Center
地铁 (Subway)：2号线、5号线雍和宫站B出口 /Exit B of Lama Temple Station, Line 2 or 5
网址 (Website)：www.bjstgy.com

皇城脚下四合院

炮局工厂青年旅舍
P.LOFT Youth Hostel
炮局胡同话沧桑
To Talk About the History in the Paoju Hutong

　　炮局工厂，一个被历史的车轮卷进战争的地方，乾隆时期用来制造大炮，抗战期间被日军用作劳工中转站，1949年以后用来生产各种电气模具……历史不容忘却，生活仍需前行，2007年底，一群饱含热情的年轻人，在废弃的工厂上建起了"炮局工厂国际青年旅舍"。这里没有奢华的装修，有的只是历史的沧桑，旅舍大门影壁后的那座炮楼，即为抗日英雄吉鸿昌被关押及就义处。如果你有时间，一定要在炮局胡同走走，触摸历史，缅怀英烈。

The artillery factory used to be a place which was involved in the war by the history. During Qianlong's reign, it was used to manufacture the artillery; during the anti-Japanese war, it was utilized by the Japanese army as a labor transit station; and after 1949, it was used to make different kinds of electric appliances and grinding tools. The history should never be forgotten, but the life shall have to go on. At the end of 2007, a group of enthusiastic young man set up on this discarded factory P. Loft Youth Hostel. There are no extravagant furnishings, but the vicissitudes of the history. The artillery tower behind the screen wall at the gate of the Hotel is the place where the anti-Japanese hero Ji Hongchang was detained and killed. If you have time, you must take a walk along the Paoju Hutong to feel the history and honor the martyrs.

地址（Add）：炮局头条29号 /29 Paoju Toutiao
电话（Tel）：8610-6402 7218
特色（Themed）：意大利餐，工厂厂房改造的房间 /Italian Cuisine, Guestrooms Altered from Industrial Buildings
地铁（Subway）：2号线、5号线雍和宫站B出口 /Exit B of Lama Temple Station, Line 2 or 5
网址（Website）：www.ploft.cn

Quadrangle Courtyards by the Imperial City Walls

北新桥周边
Beixinqiao Bridge and About

北新桥，在北京东直门内大街与雍和宫大街的交会处，地铁5号线将把你从北边的雍和宫和南边的东四快速地带到这里。过去，这里的胡同多如牛毛，所以，要想探访胡同深处的四合院，这里绝对是不容错过的好去处。

北新桥，名字叫桥，可实际上这里没有桥。既然没有桥，为什么叫北新桥呢？

据说，这里有一口古井，是北京的海眼，它被上面一个叫"江猪"的神兽镇着，一旦谁动了这口古井，北京城就有可能被涌出来的海水淹没了。

当然，这只是个传说，北新桥的古井到底在哪里，它是不是海眼，没人说得清，如果你感兴趣，就来一探究竟吧。

Beixinqiao Bridge is located at the cross of Dongzhimennei Street and Lama Temple Street, and Subway Line 5 will take you here either from the Lama Temple in the north or Dongsi in the south. There used to be numerous hutongs here, so you could not miss this place if you would like to visit the quadrangle courtyards deep in the hutongs.

There is the word bridge in Beixinqiao Bridge, but there is actually no bridge whatsoever. But why it's called bridge since there is no bridge?

It is said that there used to be an old well, the sea eye in Beijing linked to the sea. The sea eye has been guarded by "river pig", the magical beast. Once the guard was removed, the entire city would be flooded by the sea water.

Of course it is only a tale. Nobody knows where the old well is or whether it is the sea eye. Come and explore it if you are interested.

66. 醒觉咖啡 TouchWoman cafe / 90
67. 花家怡园（八爷府·花家店）Hua's Courtyard Fine Dining Restaurant / 91
68. 雍和国际青年旅舍 Lama Temple Youth Hostel / 92
69. 祥福食府 Xiangfu Restaurant / 93
70. 翼栈 Free as a Bird Restaurant & Bar / 94
71. 百合素食 BaiHe Vegetarian Food / 95
72. 花家怡园·四合院店 Hua's Courtyard Restaurant / 96
73. 吴裕泰内府菜·东直门店 Wuyutai Family Cuisine · Dongzhimen Branch / 97

皇城脚下四合院

醒觉咖啡
TouchWoman cafe
一个梦想中的私人场所
A Dreamy Private Space

　　醒觉咖啡,如同一列老式火车,满载从世界各地搜集来的古董杂货,驶向了北新胡同里的这家四合院。老北京风情融合法式乡村的随性,使这里散发着随心的能量。坐在老式窗户前,来一杯醇香的咖啡,或是尝一尝用加拿大著名品牌花草茶配制而成的奶茶,看老树落下叶子,谈情,说爱,独处,沉默……

TouchWoman café, like an old-fashioned train loaded with antiques gathered from all over the world, races towards this courtyard in Beixin Hutong. A fusion of Old Beijing's style and casualness of France's countryside, makes it a place where energy of heart exudes. Sitting in front of the old windows with a cup of mellow coffee, or watching the leaves falling from old trees and tasting milk tea prepared from well-known Canadian brand of herbal tea, here you can have a little talk about love, solitude, silence ...

地址 (Add):雍和宫大街北新胡同 38 号 /38 Beixin Hutong, Lama Temple Street
电话 (Tel):8610-8402 1928
特色 (Themed):奶茶、咖啡、意大利简餐 /Milk Tea, Coffee, Italian Meal
地铁 (Subway):2 号线、5 号线雍和宫站 C 出口 /Exit C of Lama Temple
　　　　　　　Station, Line 2 or 5
网址(Website):www.mustore.hk

花家怡园（八爷府·花家店）
Hua's Courtyard Fine Dining Restaurant
极富北京文化底蕴的高端私人会所
A Very High-end Private Club Filled with Beijing Cultural Heritage

八爷府花家店原址属于雍和宫建筑群，是雍正做皇子时雍和宫内首席御厨邬思道的宅院，乃北京为数不多保存完好的官府风格四合院。灰砖灰瓦，抄手游廊，清漆原木，石刻砖雕，虎头门踎，金鱼池，大芭蕉，合欢树，硕大的红灯笼，随风抚瓦的枝叶……传统与现代，古老与时尚，在这里奏响了和谐的乐章。雍正王朝烤鸭、翻毛月饼……官府风格渗透在八爷府花家店的血液里。

The site of Hua's Courtyard Fine Dining Restaurant used to be part of Lama Temple buildings. When Yongzheng Emperor was the prince, it belonged to Wusidao, the chief chef of Lama Temple. It is now one of Beijing's few well-preserved official style courtyards. Gray bricks and gray tiles, verandas, varnished wood, stone brick sculptures, tiger door postscripts, goldfish pond, large bananas, acacia trees, gigantic red lanterns, leaves fondling the tiles in the breeze...Traditional and modern, ancient and fashionable, all things sound together in a harmonious music movement. Yongzheng Dynasty roast duck, special moon cake, the government official style was flowing in the vein of Hua's Courtyard Fine Dining Restaurant.

地址 (Add)：北新桥头条胡同 55 号院 /55 Beixinqiao Toutiao Hutong
电话 (Tel)：8610-5128 3315
特色 (Themed)：新派北京菜、宫廷菜 /New Beijing Cuisine, Royal Cuisine
地铁 (Subway)：5 号线北新桥站 B 出口 /Exit B of Beixinqiao Station, Line 5
网址 (Website)：www.huajiacai.com

Quadrangle Courtyards by the Imperial City Walls

皇城脚下四合院

雍和国际青年旅舍
Lama Temple Youth Hostel
四合院里的跨国旅社
Transnational Hotel in the Courtyard

地址 (Add)：北新桥头条 56 号 /56 Beixinqiao Toutiao
电话 (Tel)：8610-6402 8663
地铁 (Subway)：5 号线北新桥站 B 出口 /Exit B of Beixinqiao Station, Line 5

  有胡同的地方就有四合院，就有北京记忆，就有寻找城市名片的外国朋友的身影！在北新桥头条这条北京市重点胡同文化保护区内，有一家京韵十足的旅舍——雍和国际青年旅舍。朱漆的大门、金字的门钉，老外想不进去都难。字画、对联、宫灯、盘龙……还有什么比住在这个充满了中国元素的酒店更让人动心的？雍和宫、孔庙、簋街，精神的和物质的大餐都触手可及，近距离触摸北京，就从这里开始。

Where there are hutongs, there are courtyards, there are memories of Beijing, and there are figures of foreign friends looking for the metropolitan city's business cards! In Beixinqiao Toutiao Hutong, which belongs to the key protected area of Beijing Hutong culture, there is a house full of Beijing style – Lama Temple Youth Hostel. Red lacquer doors, pitched doornails, friends from overseas cannot help going in. Paintings, couplets, lanterns, dragons ... Is there anything even more inviting than to stay in this hostel full of Chinese elements? Lama Temple, Confucian Temple, Guijie Street... Both spiritual and physical feasts are within hands' reach. Get started here with a close touch of Beijing now!

地址 (Add) : 北新桥头条 63 号 /63 Beixinqiao Toutiao
电话 (Tel) : 8610-6405 7808
特色 (Themed) : 私房菜 / Private Home Cooking
地铁 (Subway) : 5 号线北新桥站 B 出口 /Exit B of Beixinqiao Station, Line 5
网址 (Website) : www.xiangfushifu.com

祥福食府
Xiangfu Restaurant
胡同里的"裸烹"私房菜馆
A "Naked Cooking" Private Kitchen in Hutong

垂花门，影壁墙，青花瓷的鱼缸，小文鸟儿……葫芦、枣树、玉兰花儿，老北京的情调儿，精致的院儿……坐落在北新桥头条的这家祥福食府真有范儿！"裸烹"的私房菜纯天然，绝对不含添加剂。包间三个，堂食一桌，每天只接待有限的人儿。

The Festooned doors, the Chinese-style screen wall, the blue and white porcelain fish tank, the small bird...gourd, jujube tree, magnolia flowers, old Beijing style, exquisite yards...Located in Beixinqiao Toutiao Hutong, the restaurant really has a personality! The "Naked cooking" private kitchen offers dishes made from natural food, absolutely free of additives. Three private rooms, one dine-in table, the restaurant can only treat limited guests every day.

皇城脚下四合院

翼 栈
Free as a Bird Restaurant & Bar
美食江湖中驴友休憩的港湾
Gourmet Harbor Where Backpackers Can Take a Rest

　　如果你是一个地道的驴友，又喜欢香辣的美食，那就来翼栈吧。老板自己就是个想走就走的驴友，翼栈的主题当然也就成了旅行。行走八方的驴友聚集在此，谈天说地，也许下一次的旅行就又多了新的伙伴。这里的美食是湘西风味的香辣，江湖一锅鱼、翼栈哇哇哇、胡同比萨，怎样新奇怎样来。老板还是个创新美食的爱好者，说不定等你来的时候，他又研发出了新的美食！

If you are a typical backpacker who likes spicy foods, then welcome to Free as a Bird Restaurant & Bar! The boss himself is an always-ready-to-go backpacker, and traveling has naturally become the restaurant's theme. With backpackers traveling around the world gathering here chatting, you may well find new partners for the next trip. Western-Hunan style spicy food is offered here: Pot of Fish, Free as a Bird Yapping, Hutong Pizza. The boss is also an innovative cuisine lover, maybe when you come here, he's already developed some new dish!

地址 (Add)：东直门内大街北新桥头条 30 号 /30 Beixinqiao Toutiao, Dongzhimennei Street

电话 (Tel)：8610-6401 0979 / 6401 1126

特色 (Themed)：云贵湘西私房菜（江湖一锅鱼、翼栈哇哇哇、手撕包菜、动感双菇、胡同比萨）/Various Kinds of Stone Pot Dishes and Delicious Pizza

地铁 (Subway)：5 号线北新桥站 B 出口 /Exit B of Beixinqiao Station, Line 5

网址（Website）：www.freeasabird.cn

百合素食
BaiHe Vegetarian Food
与生命和谐相处之地
A Place in Harmony With Life

百合素食，一如它的名字那样古朴幽雅，在草园胡同的这座老北京四合院，曾为著名演员白杨的故居。从墨香盈洒的经典书廊走过，携满园花草的芬芳，安坐桌前，且听古琴悠远，箫音清长，品一道古茶，尝几味素菜，读几章经典，在柔缓的时光之歌中，回归和悦心性的生活。无怪乎埃及驻华大使说，在这里，可以闻到真正的中国味道。

BaiHe Vegetarian Food, with its name suggesting elegant simplicity, is located in the old-Beijing fashioned courtyard in Caoyuan hutong, the former residence of the famous actor Bai Yang. Walking through the ink scent spilled classic book gallery, carrying the fragrance of garden flowers, sitting back at the table, you can listen to the melodious Guqin and Chinese Flute, taste a cup of tea, try some vegetarian dishes, read a few chapters of classic books, going back to harmonious life in the soft and gentle song of time. No wonder the Egyptian ambassador has said here, you can smell the real Chinese scent.

地址 (Add)：东直门内北小街草园胡同甲 23 号 /23 Caoyuan Hutong, Dongzhimennei North Side Street
电话 (Tel)：8610-6405 2082
特色 (Themed)：素食菜系 /Vegetarian Diet
地铁 (Subway)：5 号线北新桥站 B 出口 /Exit B of Beixinqiao Station, Line 5
网址（Website）：www.vbaihe.com

皇城脚下四合院

花家怡园·四合院店
Hua's Courtyard Restaurant
北京餐饮的名片
The Business Card of Beijing Catering

　　与八爷府花家店的官府气质不同，花家怡园四合院店走的可是亲民路线。它地处北京著名餐饮一条街——簋街的西部，金碧辉煌的牌楼，很难让人将其与私家菜联系起来。原汁原味的四合院风貌，配上原汁原味的八旗小羊排、怡园霸王鸡、花家白菜，还有民乐演奏、变脸、捏面人，以及营业到凌晨4点的人性化服务，让你的北京之行京韵十足。

Unlike Hua's Courtyard Fine Dining Restaurant's government official style, Hua's Courtyard Restaurant gets itself closer to the ordinary people. It is located in the west of Beijing's famous food street – Guijie Street. The magnificent archway makes it hard to be linked with a private dish restaurant. Authentic courtyard style, coupled with authentic Baqi lamb chops, Hua's Chicken King, Hua's Chinese cabbage, as well as folk music, changing faces, dough figurines, and guest-friendly service till 4:00 am, making your trip to Beijing full of Beijing elements.

地址 (Add)：东直门内大街 235 号 /235 Dongzhimennei Street
电话 (Tel)：8610-5128 3315
特色 (Themed)：新派北京菜 /New Beijing Cuisine
地铁 (Subway)：5 号线北新桥站 B 出口 /Exit B of Beixinqiao Station, Line 5
网址 (Website)：www.huajiacai.com

吴裕泰内府菜·东直门店
Wuyutai Family Cuisine·Dongzhimen Branch
特色茶宴的乐享地
A Wonderful Place for Enjoying Featured Tea Party

　　吴裕泰内府菜东直门店不仅是以茶菜为核心的内务府御膳房，更是老北京老物件旧物新用的时尚引领者。在这里，老罗汉床当了餐桌，旧垂花头装饰了吊顶，旧门楼的木构件成了牌坊，琉璃瓦作了壁雕，灰瓦片勾勒出墙壁的纹理，更有收来的完整的古戏台，新打造的巨型钢铁如意……伴着一曲《高山流水》的古筝名曲，慢慢吃茶菜、品名茶、赏茶宴、观茶戏，真是人生的一大享受。

Wuyutai Family Cuisine, Dongzhimen Branch, is not only an imperial kitchen for the Household Department featuring tea dishes, but also a fashion leader who finds new uses for ancient Beijing items. Here, an old Arhat bed serves as a table. Old hanging flower heads decorate the suspended ceiling. Wooden parts of the old gate house become a memorial arch. Glazed tiles function as wall carvings. Gray tiles draw the outline of the wall texture. And there is a complete ancient stage, a newly built giant steel Ruyi... Accompanied by Mountain Stream, a famous piece of Guzheng music (Chinese zither music), you can slowly eat tea food, drink renowned tea, enjoy tea party, and watch tea plays. Indeed a great joy of life.

地址 (Add)：东直门内大街 144 号 /144 Dongzhimennei Street
电话 (Tel)：8610-6401 2228
特色 (Themed)：茶文化养生菜 /Tea Culture and Tonic Cuisine
地铁 (Subway)：5 号线北新桥站 B 出口 /Exit B of Beixinqiao Station, Line 5
　　　　　　　2 号线东直门站 D 出口 /Exit D of Dongzhimen Station, Line 2
网址（Website）：www.huajiacai.com

东四、灯市口周边
Dongsi, Dengshikou and About

　　东四，位于东城区中部，元代称十字街，明朝时在十字路口四面各建了一座木牌楼，因位居皇城之东，故称东四牌楼，简称东四。后来，牌楼虽然消失了，但东四作为地名一直沿用至今，它泛指东四南大街、东四北大街、东四西大街、朝阳门内大街交会处及附近地区。

　　灯市口，位于东城区中部，东四的南部，因明代每年农历正月初八至十八在此设灯市而得名。清代灯市移至外城，灯市口作为地名得以保留。

　　与古都中轴线平行的，是地铁5号线，它由北向南，把张自忠路、东四、灯市口这些既有年头又有看头的地区连成了片。

Located in the middle of the Dongcheng District, Dongsi was called the Cross Street in the Yuan Dynasty. In the Ming Dynasty, a three-storyed arch with four columns was constructed in all the four directions of the crossroad. It is called Dongsi (literally east four) because the four arches were located to the east of the Imperial City. Nowadays, the arches are gone, but the name Dongsi has been used since.

Dengshikou (literally lantern market) is located in the middle part of the Dongcheng District, to the south of Dongsi. During the Ming Dynasty, the lantern market was established in this area from January 8 to January 18 each lunar year. That is why it got the name of Dengshikou. The market was moved to the outer city during the Qing Dynasty, but the name for the place was kept.

Subway Line 5 runs in parallel with the ancient capital axis, and from north to south, it links the historical and wonderful Zhangzizhong Street, Dongsi and Dengshikou.

74. 皇家粮仓 Imperial Granary / 100
75. 新红资客栈 Red Capital Residence / 101
76. 天海缘四合酒店 Happy Dragon Courtyard Hostel / 102
77. 亮点设计中心 LD Design Center, LDDC / 103
78. 炒豆合作社 The Hot Bean / 104
79. 北平小院青年旅舍 Peking Yard International Hostel / 105
80. 金雅会馆（71号院）Jinya Hotel / 106
81. 甜园国际青年旅舍 Sweet Garden House / 107
82. 盛锡福中国帽文化博物馆 Sheng Xifu Museum / 108
83. 酷虾 Cool Shrimp / 109
84. 王家客栈 N.E. Hotel / 110
85. 阅微庄四合院酒店 Double Happiness Courtyard Hotel / 111
86. 四合宾馆 Sihe Courtyard Hotel / 112
87. 小院客栈 Alley Hotel / 113
88. 八十一酒店 Hotel Cote Cour Beijing / 114
89. 桂公府 Guigong's Mansion / 115
90. 史家胡同博物馆 Shijia Hutong Museum / 116
91. 细活里 SLOWLANE / 117
92. 红墙史家花园酒店 Red Wall Garden Hotel / 118
93. 婧园雅筑四合院宾馆 Jingyuan Courtyard Hotel / 119

皇城脚下四合院

皇家粮仓
Imperial Granary
演出、会议及餐饮服务的古建场所
Ancient-style Place for Performances, Conferences and Catering Services

　　皇家粮仓——南新仓，与故宫、长城、胡同、四合院齐名的文化北京的城市标签，建于明永乐七年（1409年），见证了明清24代君王、民国与1949年后的全部京都史。如今，这个昔日储存物质食粮的地方成了人们享用精神食粮的胜地。600年的皇家粮仓厅堂版昆曲《牡丹亭》在600年古仓文物遗址中，复归其表演的肇始状态。物质文化遗产与非物质文化遗产实现了完美结合。

Imperial Granary – Nanxincang, together with the Forbidden City, the Great Wall, Hutong and courtyard, are cultural labels for the city of Beijing.. Nanxincang was established in the 7th year of Yongle Emperor of Ming Dynasty. It has witnessed the entire history of Beijing's capitalhood: from 24 generations of emperors of Ming and Qing Dynasties, to the Republic of China period and post-1949 years. Today, the former "material food" storage place has become the place where people enjoy the "spiritual food". The hall version of the 600-year-old Kunqu Opera The Peony Pavilion is now performed in its very original form in the 600-year-old heritage sites of the royal granary. Here Material Cultural Heritage and Intangible Cultural Heritage achieve a perfect combination.

地址（Add）：东四十条22号 /22 Dongsi Shitiao

电话（Tel）：8610-6409 6477/6409 6499

特色（Themed）：粤菜、私房菜、烤鸭，昆曲《牡丹亭》演出
　　　　　　　　Cantonese Cuisine, Private Home Cuisine, Roast Duck; Kunqu Opera The Peony Pavilion

地铁（Subway）：2号线东四十条站D出口 /Exit D of Dongsi Shitiao Station, Line 2

网址（Website）：www.imperialgranary.com.cn

新红资客栈
Red Capital Residence
四合院里的共和国博物馆
The Museum of the Republic in the Courtyard

与其说，这是一个酒店，不如说，这是一个小型的共和国现代史博物馆。"毛主席套房"、"斯诺套房"、"韩素音套房"等5个客房环绕着四合院。毛泽东私人官邸用过的天鹅绒窗帘，周恩来用来收听国际广播的收音机，陈毅用过的红旗轿车……仿佛把你拉回到了那个红色年代。大大的会客室里珍藏着那个时代的记忆，红色革命味道十足的防空洞酒吧更是让人大开眼界。

This is not so much of a hotel; rather it is a small Modern History Museum of the Republic. "Chairman Mao Suite," "Edgar Snow Suite", "Han Suyin Suite" and so on – the five guest suites were set around the courtyard. The velvet curtains used in private residence of Mao Zedong; The radio set that Zhou Enlai used to listen to the international broadcast with; The red-flag brand car that Marshal Chen Yi rode on...As if you have been pulled back to the "red years". Memories of that era were treasured in that huge parlor; and the dugout bar filled with red revolution flavor is an eye-opener, too.

地址 (Add)： 东四六条9号 /9 Dongsi Liutiao
电话 (Tel)： 8610-8403 5303
特色 (Themed)： 小型历史博物馆 /Mini History Museum
地铁 (Subway)： 5号线张自忠路站D出口 /Exit D of Zhangzizhonglu Station, Line 5
网址 (Website)： www.redcapitalclub.com.cn

Quadrangle Courtyards by the Imperial City Walls

皇城脚下四合院

天海缘四合酒店
Happy Dragon Courtyard Hostel
四合院里话海天一线情
People from All over the Country Gather Here

地址 (Add)：东四九条 51 号 /51 Dongsi Jiutiao
电话 (Tel)：8610-8402 1970
特色 (Themed)：四合院特色客房 / Courtyard Guestrooms
地铁 (Subway)：5 号线张自忠路站 D 出口 /Exit D of Zhangzizhonglu Station, Line 5

　　天和海，一线之隔，它们既远且近。把天南海北的人聚集到一起的，是人们对四合院情有独钟的这一线情。宽敞的院落，方砖漫地，青石作阶，水墨山水诗情画意。中西合璧的客房既传统又舒适。在露台上小坐，看百年老石榴树上喜鹊搭窝，观邻居白猫在梧桐上熟睡，海天之间，独享这古城古巷的古老时光。

There is a fine line between the sky and the sea, and they are both far and near. What gathers together people from all over the country is the fondness people feel for the courtyard. With square bricks and bluestone footsteps for the spacious courtyards, the idyllic surroundings here look like an ink painting. The guestrooms are both traditional and comfortable, combining Chinese and western styles. Sitting on the balcony for a little while, you can watch magpies nest on the old pomegranate tree and the neighbor's white cat sleep tight on the plane trees and enjoy all the time spent in this ancient alley of the ancient city to yourself.

亮点设计中心
LD Design Center, LDDC
胡同里的创意工场
Creative Workshop in the Hutong

城市需要亮点，亮点需要设计。为了给北京这个古老而又现代的大都市设计出更多的亮点，在东二环内历史文化保护区，贯通东四九条的胡同里，有了一个专为设计者而设计的家——亮点五十五号创意产业园。在园区中心用三层玻璃盒子搭建的"光盒作用"办公室里，年轻设计师的各种创作灵感正在源源不断地经过"光合作用"，变成了点亮北京的一道又一道视觉冲击波。

Cities need highlights, and highlights need designs. To design more highlights for this ancient and modern metropolitan city – Beijing, in the historical and cultural protected areas in the East Second Ring Rd, through the Dongsi Jiutiao Hutong, there is a home designed specifically for designers – No.55 LD Creative Industry Park. At the center of the park there is a 3-storied glass box with the name of "light box effect" office, where all kinds of creative inspiration by young designers are being pouring through the "photosynthesis" tunnel, turning into one after another visual shock lighting Beijing up.

地址 (Add)：东四十条 94 号 /94 Dongsi Shitiao
电话 (Tel)：8610-8950 8995
特色 (Themed)：设计者的家 / Home of the Designers
地铁 (Subway)：5 号线张自忠路站 C 出口 / Exit C of Zhangzizhonglu Station, Line 5
网址 (Website)：www.lddc.com.cn

Quadrangle Courtyards by the Imperial City Walls

皇城脚下四合院

炒豆合作社
The Hot Bean
简朴烧烤小店里的中国合伙人
"Chinese Partners" in a Small, Homely Barbecue Restaurant

  炒豆合作社，一个让食客朋友们有吃，有喝，有欢笑，有回忆的餐厅！原本位于炒豆胡同，所以才有了这个让人过目不忘的店名。老板是从高中到大学的同学，他们一起玩，一起学习，一起创业，一起见证了北京胡同八年来的变化。岁月蹉跎，当年的小伙伴如今已成为了合作默契的中国合伙人，见证他们成长的，是小店里的手绘卡通、大亨果茶还有老唱片里的那一曲友谊地久天长。

The Hot Bean, a restaurant offering food, laughters, and memories for the diners! Chaodou Hutong, where its original location lies, gives the restaurant this current name. The bosses are schoolmates from high school through college. They played together, learned together, started the business together, and witnessed the changes in Beijing Hutong for the eight years together. Time flies, and the young buddies now have become "Chinese partners" who cooperate well. And what have been witnessing their growth, are the hand-drawn cartoon in the small shop, the Tycoon Beverage bottles, and old recording of the song Auld Lang Syne.

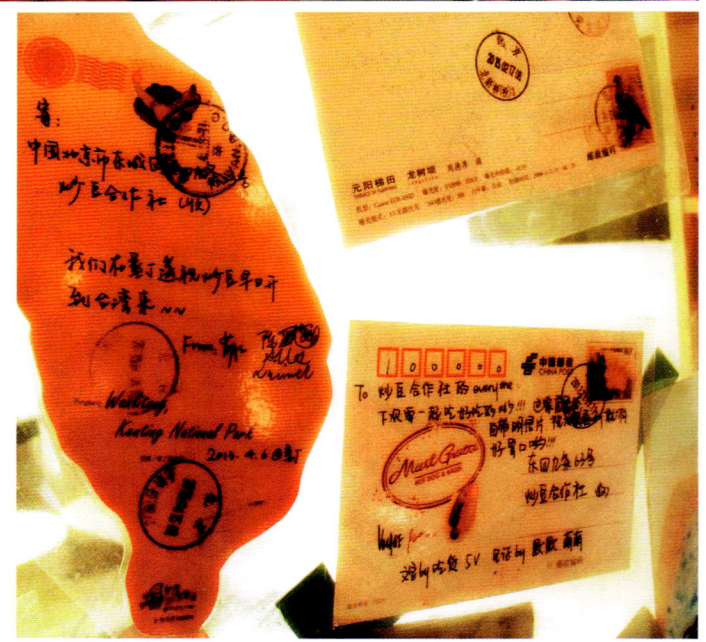

地址 (Add)：东四九条 63 号 /63 Dongsi Jiutiao
电话 (Tel)：8610-8401 0276
特色 (Themed)：特色烧烤、家常比萨 /Featured Barbeque, Home Style Pizza
地铁 (Subway)：5 号线张自忠路站 D 出口 /Exit D of Zhangzizhonglu Station, Line 5

北平小院青年旅舍
Peking Yard International Hostel
传统小院儿里体验国际范儿
Traditional Small Courtyard Providing international Experience

青板瓦，磨砖墙，大门立柱那一抹中国红，让你顿时有了家般的温暖。一把老锁，一棵老柿子树，一个提着鸟笼遛弯儿的老大爷……渐行渐远的胡同生活又慢慢走进了你的生活。在一场旅行中，如此近距离地感受古都风貌和只属于老北京的胡同生活，就在北平小院。

Green Slate tiles, grinded brick walls, door pillars with a touch of Chinese red. Together they make you suddenly feel a home-like warmth. An old lock, an old persimmon tree, a bird cage in the hand of an elderly man...The hutong life that is said be fading away, is now walking back into your life again. If you'd like to closely feel the ancient capital and the old Beijing's hutong life in your trip, Peking Yard International Hostel is your choice.

地址 (Add)：东四北大街汪芝麻胡同甲 28 号 /A 28 Wangzhima Hutong, Dongsi North Street
电话 (Tel)：8610-8404 8787
特色 (Themed)：四合院特色客房 /Courtyard Guestrooms
地铁 (Subway)：5 号线张自忠路站 D 出口 /Exit D of Zhangzizhonglu Station, Line 5
网址 (Website)：www.yhachina.com

Quadrangle Courtyards by the Imperial City Walls

皇城脚下四合院

金雅会馆（71号院）
Jinya Hotel
优雅会馆内感受京韵范儿
Feel the Old Beijing in This Elegant Hotel

这里曾是教育家吴玉章的寓所，为两个中式四合院。庭院深深，树影婆娑，在蓝天白云的掩映下如典雅的大家闺秀一般，不知心里藏了多少欢喜的忧伤的故事。推开窗，随风飘摇的落叶落在窗棂上，像起舞翻飞的蝴蝶，远处飘来的乐声直叫人怀念起那段似水的年华。

Here is the former residence of Wu Yuzhang, the famous Chinese educator. It consists of two Chinese style courtyards. With deep yards, shady trees, and in the background of a blue sky and white clouds, the hotel is just like an elegant maiden with lots of happy and sad stories in her heart. Open the window, and see the wind swaying the falling leaves onto the window frames just like dancing butterflies; and the music floating in the air makes one miss the watery time that has gone.

地址 (Add)：东四六条 71 号 /71 Dongsi Liutiao

电话 (Tel)：8610-8403 8213

特色 (Themed)：家常菜、农家菜、住宿 /Home Cooking, Farmer's Cuisine, Accommodation

地铁 (Subway)：5 号线张自忠路站 D 出口 /Exit D of Zhangzizhonglu Station, Line 5

甜园国际青年旅舍
Sweet Garden House
简约现代的四合院国际旅社
A Minimalist but Modern International Hostel in the Courtyard

地址 (Add)：东四七条 19 号 /19 Dongsi Qitiao

电话 (Tel)：8610-6405 1538

特色 (Themed)：四合院客房 / Courtyard Guestrooms

地铁 (Subway)：5 号线张自忠路站 C 出口 /Exit C of Zhangzizhonglu Station, Line 5

　　在东四七条北京重点胡同文化保护区内，人们经常能够看到三三两两的国内外背包客和自助游人士行走在古老的街巷里。说不定，其中就有几个一抬脚进了这家能够提供英语服务的 19 号小院。这里精巧、别致，甜蜜、温馨，不负它甜园之名。

In Dongsi Qitiao Hutong, which is part of Beijing Hutong culture key protected areas, backpackers from in and outside the country are often seen walking in the old streets and alleys in twos and threes. Maybe among them, some have stepped into the No. 19 courtyard where English service is available. Delicate and chic, sweet and warm, it lives up to the Hostel name – Sweet Garden.

皇城脚下四合院

盛锡福中国帽文化博物馆
Sheng Xifu Museum
中国第一家冠帽文化博物馆
The First Hat Culture Museum in China

老北京有句顺口溜：头戴盛锡福，脚蹬内联升，身穿瑞蚨祥，腰缠四大恒。这"头戴盛锡福"，说的就是盛锡福的帽子。为了展示中国历史悠久的帽文化，百年老字号制帽店"盛锡福"在东四北大街筹建了中国帽文化博物馆。博物馆从通辽出土的4600年前的骨冠说起，将不同时代有代表性的冠帽一一呈现在参观者面前。人们不但可以观看展品，还有机会看到国家级非物质文化遗产传承人李金善现场制帽。

"It is distinguished to wear a Shengxifu hat, a pair of Neiliansheng boots, clothes made from Ruifuxiang silks and satins, and carry with you banknotes of the four largest private Chinese-style banks." An old Beijing doggerel goes. Sheng Xifu hat is what is referred to here. In order to display the long history of the hat culture of China, "Sheng Xifu", the time-honored hat shop established the China Hat Heritage Museum in north Dongsi Avenue. From the bone hat unearthed in Tongliao which dates back to 4600 years ago, representative hats of different times are presented in front of the visitors. Visitors can not only appreciate the exhibits but also have a chance to watch Li Jinshan, a national intangible cultural heritage inheritor, make hats at the scene.

地址 (Add)：东四北大街368号 /368 Dongsi North Street
电话 (Tel)：8610-6407 6488
特色 (Themed)：冠帽 /Hat, 周末闭馆 /Closed on Weekends
地铁 (Subway)：5号线、6号线东四站B出口 /Exit B of Dongsi Station, Line 5 or 6
网址 (Website)：www.shengxifu.com.cn

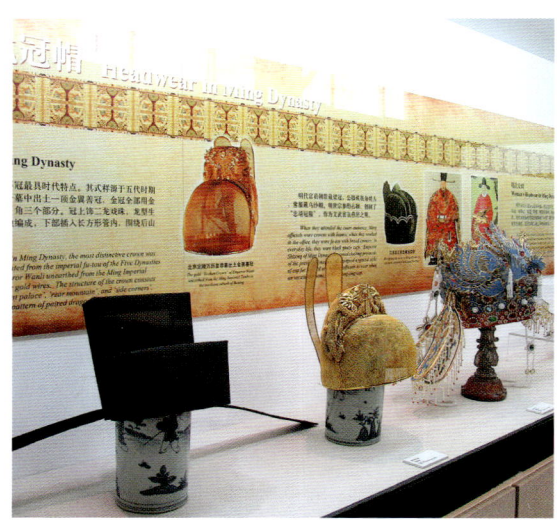

酷 虾
Cool Shrimp
京城唯一一家以做虾肴为特色的湖南菜馆
The Only Hunan Cuisine Restaurant in Beijing Featuring Shrimp Dishes

　　美食最乡思。胡同深处，味之江湖，前清造币厂的一个院子里，一款闭月羞花的虾肴高调登场，让爱虾一族大呼过瘾！紧接着登场的是青椒水煮虾，鲜香爽滑，脆嫩弹齿。老长沙口味虾、酥麻虾、蒜香虾，每个菜品都拥有一众食客粉丝。招牌功夫主打虾，二十四种做法，二十四种味道，人生百味，尽在其中……

Gourmet food embodies homesickness. Located in a yard of a Qing dynasty mint deep in the hutong, a delicious shrimp dish is prepared to the full satisfaction of fans of shrimp dishes. Then comes the green pepper boiled shrimps, with fresh, smooth, crisp and tender taste. Each shrimp dish, for example, the old Changsha flavor shrimp, crisp shrimp and garlic shrimp, has a group of fans. Shrimp dishes are its specialty and can be prepared in 24 different ways in 24 flavors, absorbing all tastes of life...

老长沙口味虾　　68元/份
主料：小龙虾
辅料：中草药香料
味型：鲜香猛辣

地址 (Add)：东四四条甲 83 号 /A 83 Dongsi Sitiao
电话 (Tel)：8610-6405 4904
特色 (Themed)：虾肴湘菜馆 /Shrimp Hunan Cuisine Restaurant
地铁 (Subway)：5 号线、6 号线东四站 B 出口 /Exit B of Dongsi Station, Line 5 or 6

皇城脚下四合院

王家客栈
N.E. Hotel
家一样的住所
A Place Like Home

　　王家客栈，听名字，就知道这是一家亲切中透着温馨的家庭式住所。走入月牙胡同，远远望过去，两个大红灯笼高高挂起，雕梁画栋的大门上写着"王家客栈"几个字。推门而入，中国风扑面而来——古玩字画，太师椅，中国红，中国结，充满文化气息而又温馨的装饰让人立刻有了回家的感觉。如果有雅兴，跟中国师傅耍上几趟太极拳，你一定不虚此行！

The name Wang's inn sounds like a warm and cozy home. Walking into the Yueya (cresent) Hutong and looking from afar, you can see two red lanterns hanging up high and at the door of a richly ornamented building, which reads "Wang's Inn". Open the door and come in, you will be embraced by items in Chinese style such as antique calligraphy and painting, old-fashioned wooden armchairs, Chinese red, and Chinese knot. All the decorations are full of cultural atmosphere and warmth, which immediately make you feel like home. If you have refined interest to do several rounds of shadowboxing, you can learn from the Chinese teachers, thus highlighting your entire trip.

地址 (Add)：东四六条月牙胡同 10 号院 /10 Yueya Hutong, Dongsi Liutiao
电话 (Tel)：8610-6402 1671
特色 (Themed)：中式特色客房 /Featured Guestrooms in Chinese Courtyard
地铁 (Subway)：5 号线张自忠路站 C 出口 /Exit C of Zhangzizhonglu Station, Line 5
网址（Website）：www.nehotelbj.com

阅微庄四合院酒店
Double Happiness Courtyard Hotel
在纪晓岚宅院里感受传统文化的魅力
Feel the Charm of Traditional Culture in Ji Xiaolan's House

眼前这个两进的四合院，曾是清代大学士纪晓岚（昀）的外宅，如今，寻常百姓也能在这里住上个三日五日，闻一闻那大烟袋里残存的烟草味儿。阅微庄四合院酒店最大限度保留了传统四合院的风貌，全部摆设采用仿制的明清家具，随处可见的字画和古董，各种有趣的小玩意和民族工艺饰品，都展现出古都文化的魅力。

This quadrangle courtyard house with two courtyards is the former residence of Ji Xiaolan(yun), the Grand Secretary in the Qing dynasty. Nowadays, ordinary people can also live here for several days and smell the remaining tobacco flavor in that big tobacco pouch. Double Happiness Courtyard Hotel has retained the features of traditional courtyard houses to the maximum and all the furnishings here are imitative of Ming and Qing dynasties' furniture. Calligraphy works, paintings and antiques are seen everywhere and all kinds of interesting gadgets as well as ethnic craft ornaments show the charm of the ancient capital's culture.

地址 (Add)：东四四条 37 号 /37 Dongsi Sitiao
电话 (Tel)：8610-6400 7762
特色 (Themed)：中式两进四合院特色客房 /Featured Guestrooms With Two Chinese Courtyard
地铁 (Subway)：5 号线东四站 B 出口 /Exit B of Dongsi Station, Line 5
网址 (Website)：www.hotel37.com

皇城脚下四合院

四合宾馆
Sihe Courtyard Hotel
京城唯一一家始于清代前期的三进式四合院宾馆
The Only Courtyard Hotel With Three Courtyards Dated Back to Early Qing Dynasty

  北京的历史，是用四合院里寻常百姓的生活写就的，有了他们，这个城市才鲜活灵动起来。在灯草胡同，有一个三进四合院，最早是皇室贵族的住所，后来成为京剧大师梅兰芳先生的故居。院落自然古朴，秀丽天成，下榻于此，游走于花团锦簇中，不免生出故人已逝的感慨，唯有门口一对汉白玉石狮，仍守望着逝去的岁月。

The history of Beijing is made up of the ordinary people's life in courtyard houses. The city is full of life because of them. In Dengcao Hutong, there is a courtyard house with three courtyards which originally served as the residence of the royal family and later became the former residence of Mei Lanfang, the Beijing Opera master. The house is characterized by natural simplicity and beauty. Living here and wandering among blossoms will inevitably trigger memories of the deceased. Only a pair of white marble stone lions at the gate bears witness to the past.

地址 (Add)：东四南大街灯草胡同 5 号 /5 Dengcao Hutong, Dongsi South Street

电话 (Tel)：8610-5169 3555

特色 (Themed)：三进式老北京四合院特色客房 /Featured Guestrooms With Three Chinese Courtyards

地铁 (Subway)：5 号线、6 号线东四站 C 出口 /Exit C of Dongsi Station, Line 5 or 6

网址 (Website)：www.sihehotel.com

小院客栈
Alley Hotel
百年老街看宅门往事
Observe the Past Through an Ancient Street

"百年老街"礼士胡同，可是条藏龙卧虎的巷子，大宅子多，故事也多。清朝宰相刘墉故第就在胡同西头，印尼驻华大使馆也曾落户于此，电视剧《大宅门》也是在129号院拍的外景。小院客栈，这个名字很低调但历史积淀很深厚的酒店，就在这个有年头的胡同里。胡同中部路北墙上有十几块精美绝伦的大幅清代砖雕，这是在故宫都找不到的宝贝，您不妨按下快门，把老北京老胡同的记忆带回家！

The time-honored Lishi Hutong is an alley where big houses as well as stories abound. At the west end of the hutong lies the former residence of Liu Yong, a Prime Minister of the Qing Dynasty. The Indonesian embassy was once located here, too. The Grand Mansion Gate, a popular Chinese TV series, is shoot in the No.129 house for outdoor scenes. Alley hotel, a very low-key but historical hotel is situated in this ancient alley. There is more than a dozen pieces of exquisite Qing Dynasty tiles carving on the north wall in the middle of the hutong, which are rarities not to be found even in the Forbidden City. Press the shutter and take home the memory of ancient Beijing hutongs!

地址 (Add)：礼士胡同 12 号 /12 Lishi Hutong
电话 (Tel)：8610-6521 2508/6521 2658
特色 (Themed)：中式特色客房 /Featured Guestrooms in Chinese Courtyard
地铁 (Subway)：2/5/6 号线朝阳门站 H 出口、东四站 C 出口 / Exit H of Chaoyangmen Station or Exit C of Dongsi Station, Line 2/5/6
网址 (Website)：www.alleyhotel.com

皇城脚下四合院

八十一酒店
Hotel Cote Cour Beijing
谱写古典与时尚的协奏曲
Compose a Concerto of the Classical and Fashion

  建筑，是凝固的音乐；音乐，是活化的建筑。演乐胡同里的一砖一瓦，奏响的分明是那老北京记忆深处的小夜曲。似水流年，留声机把我们拉回到了明朝，耳边传来宫廷乐师彩排演奏的乐符，音乐的休止符停留在了一个虚掩的朱漆大门前，八十一酒店·演乐店向您敞开了大门。古典风格中跳动着时尚的音符，中西合璧，古今混搭，让您在北京昔日的风华中感受当代设计的品位。

地址 (Add)：东四南大街演乐胡同 70 号 /70 Yanyue Hutong, Dongsi South Street

电话 (Tel)：8610-6523 9598

特色 (Themed)：杭州菜系、中西合璧客房 /Hangzhou Cuisine, Guestroom With Chinese and Western Elements

地铁 (Subway)：5 号线、6 号线东四站 C 出口 /Exit C of Dongsi Station, Line 5 or 6

网址 (Website)：www.hotelcotecourbj.com

Architecture is frozen music, and music, living architecture. What the bricks and tiles of Yanyue Hutong plays is a serenade deep in the memories of old Beijing. As time goes by, phonograph brings us back to the Ming Dynasty. Notes played by court musicians at rehearsal is heard, and the pause of the music stays in front of a big red door left unlocked, opening to Hotel Cote Cour Beijing, Yanyue Branch. With fashion notes beating in the classical style, Chinese and western styles are blended, and ancient and modern styles are mixed, enabling you to feel the contemporary design taste in the past elegance of Beijing.

桂公府
Guigong's Mansion
一门二后的凤凰窝
A "Phenix Nest", Home of Two Empresses

桂公府作为北京现存的唯一一座皇后宅邸，因主人是慈禧太后的弟弟承恩公桂祥而得名。它见证了古都百年的变更与传奇，慈禧唯一一次归省是在这里，隆裕皇后大婚出阁亦在这里。一门二后的故事在京城是绝无仅有的，也让其"凤凰窝"的美誉不胫而走，直至今日，这里依然是人们心中为婚嫁祈福的吉祥之地。

Guigong's Mansion, as the only existing mansion of the queens' family, got its name for the fact that it was owned by Gui Xiang, or Cheng'en, the brother of the Empress Dowager Cixi. It witnessed the changes and legends of the ancient capital through centuries. It was the home where Empress Dowager Cixi returned for the visit after marriage and where Empress Dowager Longyu got married. A family producing two empresses is the only one of its kind in the capital city, earning the family mansion the reputation of "phoenix nest". Until today, it is still considered a propitious place for marriage blessing.

地址 (Add)：朝内南小街大方家胡同芳嘉园 11 号 /11 Fangjiayuan, Dafangjia Hutong, Chaoyangmennei South Side Street

电话 (Tel)：8610-8511 2223/6522 5504

特色 (Themed)：宫廷菜（慈禧家宴）、粤菜、烤鸭 / Royal Cuisine (Cixi Family Feast), Cantonese Cuisine, Roast Duck

地铁 (Subway)：2 号线、6 号线朝阳门站 G、H 出口 / Exit G or H of Chaoyangmen Station, Line 2 or 6

皇城脚下四合院

史家胡同博物馆
Shijia Hutong Museum
咱老百姓自己的博物馆
Folk Museum for Folks

　　北京的根，在胡同里；胡同的根，在四合院的一砖一瓦里，在老百姓的生活里……如今，这一砖一瓦铺进了老百姓自己的博物馆里。胡同里的叫卖声，老街坊的旧物件，还有那从建筑垃圾里"抢救"来的老砖头，也都一一保存在了这个博物馆里，这就是北京人艺的摇篮，近代教育的发端，人文荟萃的宝巷——史家胡同里的博物馆。走进去，胡同、四合院在展柜里，在影像里；走出来，希望胡同、四合院永远在现实世界里。

Beijing takes root in the Hutong, the Hutong take root in the bricks and tiles of the courtyards. In this folk museum, you will see the ancient bricks and tiles rescued from the modern construction waste, the old articles collected from the neighborhoods, and listen toold ditty from the hawkers. Exhibition rooms will show you the development of Chinese modern education, Beijing People's Art Theatre, Celebrities from the Lane, etc. Inside the museum, lanes and courtyards are in the images and show rooms; outside the museum, we hope the lanes and courtyards will stand always in the real world.

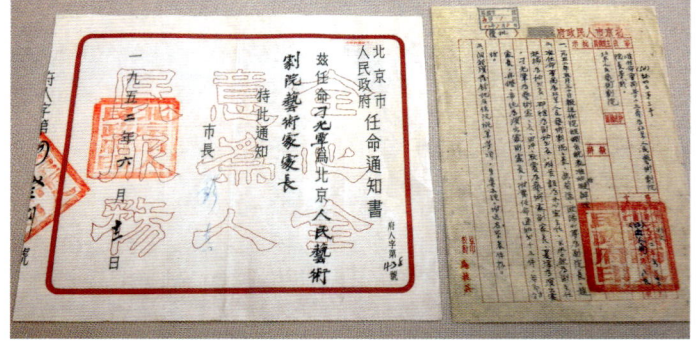

地址 (Add)：史家胡同 24 号 /24 Shijia Hutong
电话 (Tel)：8610-6525 2505
特色 (Themed)：免费 /Free，周一闭馆 /Closed on Mondays
地铁 (Subway)：5 号线灯市口站 C 出口 /Exit C of Dengshikou Station, Line 5

— Quadrangle Courtyards by the Imperial City Walls —

细活里
SLOWLANE
史家胡同里的慢生活
Slow Life in Shijia Hutong

　　精工出细活！"细活里"，一家仰仗中国传统的生活哲学，通过精心设计，用中国最传统的工艺，做出最时尚经典的家庭和生活用品的小店，沐浴在史家胡同浓浓的人文气息中。完全的手工制作，赋予每件器物独特的生命力，没有过度的包装，没有华丽的外表，不进行批量生产，只做专属于你的那个它。用爱，加工；用心，生活。来细活里，感受悦己怡人的生活方式！

Slow work makes perfection! SLOWLANE, a shop which relies on the traditional Chinese philosophy of life, makes the most fashionable and classical household and daily life items through elaborate design and with China's traditional craft, is bathed in profound cultural atmosphere of Shijia Hutong. Completely handmade, each item is endowed with unique vitality, with no excessive packaging, no gorgeous appearance and is not for mass production. They only make it exclusively for you. Their motto is to make every item with love and to live wholeheartedly. Come here and feel way of life that pleases both yourself and others.

地址 (Add)：史家胡同 13 号 /13 Shijia Hutong
电话 (Tel)：8610-6522 7770
特色 (Themed)：传统手工艺店 /Traditional Craftsmanship Shop
地铁 (Subway)：5 号线灯市口站 C 出口 /Exit C of Dengshikou Station, Line 5

皇城脚下四合院

红墙史家花园酒店
Red Wall Garden Hotel
胡同里的文化走廊
A Cultural Corridor in the Hutong

地址 (Add)：史家胡同 41 号 /41 Shijia Hutong
电话 (Tel)：8610-5169 2222
特色 (Themed)：养生菜、家常菜、红墙院景房 /Tonic Foods, Home Cooking; Garden View Room
地铁 (Subway)：5 号线灯市口站 C 出口 /Exit C of Dengshikou Station, Line 5
网址（Website）：www.rwghotel.com

一条老胡同，一曲"史家"的绝唱，唱出了人们对老北京风情的深深眷恋，唱出了红墙史家花园酒店的中国味儿。典型的四合院式结构把 40 多套景观大宅围合在一起，琉璃黄的门庭，长城灰的地面，玉脂白的饰面，国槐绿的植物，原木色的窗栏凳架，在中国红的基调中诉说着老北京的万千风情。

Located in an old hutong, the Red Wall Garden Hotel's Chinese style and flavor are fully expressed by a song which embodies the nostalgia of people toward ancient Beijing flavor. It's typical courtyard architectural structure has enclosed in it more than 40 landscaped mansions. The coloured glaze yellow gate, Great Wall grey ground, jade white finish, Chinese scholar tree, burly wood window frame and stools in Chinese red convey the stunning beauty and style of the ancient Beijing.

婧园雅筑四合院宾馆
Jingyuan Courtyard Hotel
繁华商业街巷里的雅致小院
An Elegant Courtyard in the Prosperous Commercial Street

当你漫步在北京最繁华的商业步行街——王府井时，可曾留意过在距新东安市场仅几步之遥，有一处雅致的四合院静静伫立在天主教堂南侧，清末朝廷重臣左宗棠曾居于此，后来，这里成为北京基督教女青年会开展公益事业的地方。想要近距离感受老北京文化的朋友，不妨到此小住几日，跟着中国师傅耍上几趟太极拳，或是享受中国剪纸带来的那份内心的宁静。

Strolling in Wangfujing, the most prosperous commercial pedestrian street in Beijing, you would have ever paid heed to an elegant courtyard house, which, just a few steps away from Beijing AMP (formerly known as Xin Dong An Plaza), stands quietly to the south of the Christianity church. Tso Tsungtang (1812-1885), an important official of late Qing Dynasty, once resided here. Later, the courtyard house served as the place where Beijing Young Women's Christian Association organized public welfare activities. If you want to have a close contact with the culture of old Beijing, just live for several days in our hotel, where you can play shadowboxing together with Chinese masters, or immerse in the tranquility brought by Chinese paper cutting.

地址 (Add)：王府井西堂子胡同 35 号 /35 Xitangzi Hutong, Wangfujing
电话 (Tel)：8610-6525 9259
特色 (Themed)：中式特色客房 /Featured Guestrooms in Chinese Courtyard
地铁 (Subway)：5 号线灯市口站 A 出口 /Exit A of Dengshikou Station, Line 5
网址 (Website)：www.ywcagardenhotel.com.cn

前门周边
Qianmen and About

从天安门广场一路向南，在古都中轴线上，是北京著名的商业街——前门大街。京城建外城前，这里是皇帝出城赴天坛祭天的御路，建外城后，这里就成了外城最主要的街道，临街出现了鲜鱼口、猪（珠）市口、煤市口、粮食店等集市。

如今的前门特色商业街老字号林立，繁华不减当年。

为出行方便，我们将周边的几家四合院特色服务设施也整合在了这条线路里。

Further south to the Tiananmen Square and along the ancient city axis, there are the famous business street called Qianmen Street. Before the outer city was built, this street was the royal route to the Temple of Heaven where the Emperor offered sacrifice for the Heaven. When the outer city was built, it became the main street where there were various markets for fish, pigs, coal, grains and so on.

Now the Qianman Business Street is full of famous traditional business, as prosperous as they used to be.

To make the trip to Qianmen easy, this guide book includes several courtyard hotels with special services in this route.

94. 利群烤鸭店 Liqun Roast Duck Restaurant / 122
95. 壹条龙饭庄 Yitiaolong Restaurant / 123
96. 都一处 Duyichu Restaurant / 124
97. 皇家驿栈·前门店 The Emperor · Qianmen Branch / 125
98. 泉谷酒店 Springs Valley / 126
99. 金台夕照会馆 Xizhao Temple Hotel / 127
100. 东城区第二图书馆外借处 Dongcheng District Second Library / 128

皇城脚下四合院

利群烤鸭店
Liqun Roast Duck Restaurant
在幽静胡同尝美味烤鸭
Taste Delicious Roast Duck in the Quiet Hutong

　　在前门的胡同里,到处都是古色古香的历史沉淀,突然,一股烤鸭的馨香飘然而至。胡同里,老旧的院门前,一块方形的石头,上刻"利群"两字,这里就是有名的利群烤鸭店。胡同虽小,却难抵诱人香;门脸不大,仍招徕八方客。不管是耄耋的老北京,还是朝气的旅游客,给这个原本幽静的小胡同增添了一抹生气,真的是"小处藏有大风景,为有馨香招人来"!

In the hutongs of Qianmen area, the sense of history and antiquity can be felt everywhere. All of a sudden, a fragrant smell of the roast duck emerges. In the hutong, there is a square stone engraved with the two characters "Li Qun" in front of an old courtyard door. Here is the famous Liqun Roast Duck Restaurant. Though it is not a spacious hutong, its smell of fragrance is irresistible. Though it is a small restaurant, it attracts diners from all over the country and the world. Both old Beijinese and new tourists have injected new life to the originally quiet hutong. The fragrant smell of roast duck explains the throngs of diners.

地址 (Add): 前门东大街草厂三条北翔凤胡同 /Beixiangfeng Hutong, Caochang Santiao, Qianmen East Street

电话 (Tel): 8610-6705 5578 / 6702 5681

特色 (Themed): 烤鸭、特色烤鸭菜(芥末鸭掌、盐水鸭肝等) Roast Duck, Specialties (Duck Feet With Mustard, Boiled Duck Liver With Salt)

地铁 (Subway): 2号线前门站B出口 /Exit B of Qianmen Station, Line 2

壹条龙饭庄
Yitiaolong Restaurant
在龙降之地品纯正涮肉
Savor the Best Boiled Meat at the Restaurant Which Once Received the Emperor

在熙熙攘攘的前门大街上，一个三层小楼优雅别致，独特的清代庭院风格给人耳目一新的感觉。这里，就是大名鼎鼎的老字号"壹条龙饭庄"。金字招牌上遒劲有力的"壹条龙"几个字书写着它的沧桑和辉煌，现代化的经营理念释放着它的活力和光芒。曾经，它让光绪帝胃口大开；如今，寻常百姓常来这里犒劳自己。

In the bustling Qianmen Street, there is an elegant three-storeyed building whose unique style of the Qing Dynasty courtyard leaving people an impression of being new and fresh. This is the famous time-honored brand "Yitiaolong Restaurant". The characters "Yitiaolong" (meaning one dragon) on the gold-lettered signboard have witnessed its vicissitudes of life and past glories, and its modern management concept has released its vitality and radiance. Once upon a time, it whetted the appetite of Emperor Guangxu; nowadays, ordinary people frequent the restaurant to treat themselves.

地址 (Add)：前门大街 27 号 /27 Qianmen Street
电话 (Tel)：8610-6304 4638
特色 (Themed)：老北京火锅 /Traditional Beijing Hotpot
地铁 (Subway)：2 号线前门站 C 出口 /Exit C of Qianmen Station, Line 2

皇城脚下四合院

都一处
Duyichu Restaurant
品百年烧卖 感美食文化
Feel the Delicacy Culture in a Taste of the Time-honored Shaomai

　　在北京古都中轴线上，有的不只是皇家的建筑，还有皇家的美味。在前门大街，一座三层小楼，抬头三个大字"都一处"，这就是前门有名的烧卖老店。相传，乾隆对这里的烧卖赞不绝口，御赐店名"都一处"。"都城老铺烧卖王，一块皇匾赐辉煌。处地临街多贵客，鲜香味美共来尝。"想要品尝老店烧卖的人，一定不要错过这里。

There are not only royal architectures but also places of the royal dainties around the central axis of the ancient capital Beijing. In Qianmen Street, if you look up to a three-storeyed building, you will find three characters "Duyichu" on a signboard. This is the famous time-honored shaomai a steamed dimsum with sticky rice stuffing restaurant in the Qianmen area. It is said that Emperor Qianlong lauded the shaomai here and granted the name "Duyichu". As an ancient poem goes, "The shaomai here ranks top in the capital city of Beijing, and it is a glory that the emperor granted a signboard. It is frequented by distinguished guests who want to taste the fresh and fragrant delicacy." For those who want to taste delicate shaomai, Duyichu Restaurant is a must-go restaurant that you cannot miss.

地址 (Add)：前门大街 38 号 /38 Qianmen Street
电话 (Tel)：8610-6702 4578
特色 (Themed)：鲁菜、烧卖 /Shandong Cuisine, Steamed Dumpling With the Dough Gathered at the Top
地铁 (Subway)：2 号线前门站 B 出口 /Exit B of Qianmen Station, Line 2

皇家驿栈·前门店
The Emperor·Qianmen Branch
京城首家"水"文化创意精品酒店
The First Water Culture Creative Boutique Hotel in Beijing

在前门大街老字号浴池——兴华池的原址上,正在演绎着一场"上善若水,连接天地"的水文化大戏,戏的主角便是皇家驿站·前门店。作为京城首家"水"文化创意精品酒店,独特的"水"元素在店内四处浮现。食珍馐品佳酿,观往来车水马龙、鸿儒白丁,虽无流觞曲水之惬意,却亦足以畅叙幽情,更可携着此番诗情画意观赏陈列在画廊中的艺术品。

At the site of Xinghuachi, a former bathing pool in Qianmen street, there stands The Emperor, the leading role in the water culture drama best described "as good as water, connecting heaven and earth". As the first "water" culture creative boutique hotel in the city, the unique "water" element can be felt all over the hotel. Here you can taste delicacies as well as vintage wine, observe the flow of traffic, meet learned scholars or commoners. With the poetic sentiment, you can appreciate the artworks displayed in the gallery.

地址 (Add):前门商业区鲜鱼口街 87 号 /87 Xianyukou Street, Qianmen Commercial Area
电话 (Tel):8610-6701 7790
特色 (Themed):"水"文化创意精品酒店 /Water Culture Creative Boutique Hotel
地铁 (Subway):2 号线前门站 B 出口 /Exit B of Qianmen Station, Line 2
网址 (Website):www.theemperor.com.cn

皇城脚下四合院

泉谷酒店
Springs Valley
在现代之地体味传统文化
Savoring Traditional Culture in Modern Land

　　泉，是生命和活力的象征；谷，是泉的发源地，泉谷酒店由此得名。整个酒店于时尚中凸显中国文化的悠远和厚重，置身其中，品一杯香茗，中国悠远的文化气息扑面而来，幽静而恬淡的感觉由心而生，瞬间就荡涤了疲劳和喧嚣。繁忙的都市人，在你累了的时候，不妨到此清幽处小住几日，给身体和心灵一个放松的谷地。

The spring water, is a symbol of life and vitality; the valley, is the birthplace of springs. This is where the name of Spring Valley comes from. The entire hotel highlights the distance and richness of the Chinese culture in a fashionable way. Being in here, a cup of tea in hand, feeling Chinese culture blowing to your face, a sense of quietude and tranquility will rise from your heart, and fatigue and bustle will be instantly wiped up. Busy city people, when you are feeling tired, you may just spend a few days at this quiet place, to relax the body and mind in this carefree valley.

地址 (Add)：幸福大街 57 号 /57 Xingfu Street

电话 (Tel)：8610-6741 1116

特色 (Themed)：新西兰羊排，豪华主题套房 /New Zealand Lamb, Luxury Theme Suite

地铁 (Subway)：5 号线天坛东门 B 出口，换乘公交 6/35 路北京体育馆站 Exit B of Tiantandongmen Station, Line 5, Then Transfer to Bus 6/35 to Beijingtiyuguan Station

金台夕照会馆
Xizhao Temple Hotel
让心放飞在禅意的北京
Let Your Heart Fly in Zen Beijing

金台夕照，昔日的"燕京八景"之一，春秋战国时期燕昭王为招纳天下贤士而修建的黄金台，如今，已变身成着力打造"禅意、诗意、适意"意境的文化主题酒店。您来到这里，洗去一身疲累，听泠泠琴声，可处清都之地而远烦忧；细品禅茶，一啜一饮间，于造化中而近天然。偶食佛家素斋，清珍淡馐，和胃养生益好年；闲看百年槐荫，自在窗前，参透禅机得欣然。

"Jintai Xizhao" is one of the former "Eight Great Sceneries in old Beijing". This Gold Terrace built by the Zhao King of Yan State in the Spring and Autumn Period, has now become the "Zen, poetic and agreeable" mood of the new culture theme hotel. When you come here, you can wash away the fatigue, listen to euphonious melodies, forget about all the worries and cares; You can taste the tea in the mood of Zen, and between sips of drink, get yourself closer to nature. The Buddhist vegetarian food here, plain but delicate, is good for your health. Take a leisurely look at the shade of pagoda trees through the window, reading the pith of Zen in absolute comfort.

Quadrangle Courtyards by the Imperial City Walls

地址 (Add)：夕照寺中街 15 号 /15 Xizhaosi Middle Street
电话 (Tel)：8610-6711 9999
特色 (Themed)：官府菜 /Royal Cuisine
地铁 (Subway)：5 号线崇文门站换乘公交 12 路夕照寺北口站 Chongwenmen Station, Line 5, Transfer to Bus 12 to Xizhaosibeikou Station
网址 (Website)：www.king-talenthotel.com

皇城脚下四合院

东城区第二图书馆外借处
Dongcheng District Second Library
在弹丸雅室博览古今文化
Browsing Ancient and Modern Cultures in the Small but Elegant Room

崇文门外的花市大街，旧时说书、卖艺、卖年糕的地儿，受火德真君庙里的火神庇佑，老百姓的生意做得红红火火。现如今，这座小庙被原崇文区图书馆借用，成为了一处在历史的建筑里品味历史的新去处。来到这个用铁栅栏围起来的古老建筑前，推开红漆大门，一股淡淡的书香扑面而来，穿行其间，屏蔽掉喧嚣，让人立刻就有了阅读的欲望，拿一本书，细细咀嚼，整个世界都静了下来。这真是"弹丸之地藏雅室，弹指之间阅古今"！

In the old times, on the Flower Market Street in Chongwenmenwai area, storytellers, entertainers, peddlers selling cakes, all their businesses boomed, thanks to the blessing from the God of fire in the nearby Huodezhenjun temple. Now, utilized by Chongwen District Library, the temple has become a new place where you can taste the history right in a historic building. Standing before the iron-fenced old building, opening the gates with red paint, going through the courtyard, feeling the scent of books, blocking out the noise from the outside world, people immediately have a desire to read. Take a book and chew it, and the whole world becomes silent. Just like the poem lyrics go, "In a tiny place elegant rooms are hidden; and through the fingers history is traced!"

地址 (Add)：西花市大街 113 号 /113 Xihuashi Street
电话 (Tel)：8610-6712 4728
地铁 (Subway)：5 号线崇文门站 C 出口 /Exit C of Chongwenmen Station, Line 5
网址 (Website)：www.cwlib.com

当您来到王府井大街、前门大街、南锣鼓巷游览时，手机可以充当您的"导游"啦！轻轻拨动一下手指，即可迅速掌握京城第一商业街的热门潮店、知晓御路天街的前世今生，了解元代风貌胡同里的名人逸事……详见使用说明。

When you go touring in Wangfujing St, Qianmen St and Nanluoguxiang Alley, the mobile phone can play the role of your "guide". By moving the tip of your finger you will get to know the popular stores in the No.1 commercial street, the history of the imperial street and the nobilities and their anecdotes in the hutongs which still bear the style and features in the Yuan Dynasty. See details in the usage directions.

东城区自助旅游指南
DIY Tourist Guide to Beijing Dongcheng Distrct

VISIT BEIJING

提示：本WiFi为局域网，不提供Internet服务。
Tips: Internet service is unavailable in this WIFI access point.

1. 请使用运营商网络在应用商店中下载"东城旅游"客户端程序。
Step1: For "Dongcheng Tourism" client download, please go to APP STORE via other networks.

扫描此二维码获取IOS版　　扫描此二维码获取安卓版

2. 请打开手机WiFi，搜索并连接Visit Beijing；连接以后，可以在"东城旅游"客户端中免费下载旅游资讯包。这是免费的。
Step 2: Search and connect to: Visit Beijing. Download the Tourism Info Package in "Dongcheng Tourism" client. It's free.

北京市东城区旅游发展委员会
Dongcheng District Commission of Tourism Development of Beijing Municipality

提供"东城旅游电子资讯包"下载服务的四合院商家
"Electronic Information Package of Dongcheng Tourism" Download Available

名称	Name	页码 (Page)
秦唐府七号院	Courtyard 7	47
侣松园宾馆	Lvsongyuan Hotel	31
都一处·前门店	Duyichu Restaurant · Qianmen Branch	124
文宇奶酪	Wenyu Cheese	43
咂摸餐吧	Taste Restaurant	34
创可贴T恤	Plastered T-shirts	41
老舍纪念馆	Lao She Memorial Hall	19
盛锡福中国帽文化博物馆	Sheng Xifu Museum	108

特别提示
正规旅行社不允许在街头散发旅游小广告，不在北京交通地图上刊登广告，不利用公交站牌发布旅游信息和小名片。

旅游途中，请记下您乘坐的旅游车牌号及相关证据，以备维权使用。

Special Tips
A regular tourist service is not allowed to distribute small ads in the street, carry ads in the Beijing Traffic Map and publicize any tourist information or name card on the road traffic signs.

During your journey please note down the plate number of your tour bus and relevant evidence for possible use in protecting your rights.

索引

A 埃蒙小镇 / 84

B 八十一酒店 / 114
百合素食 / 95
宝月出品 / 60
北平小院青年旅舍 / 105

C 猜火车电影餐厅 / 83
炒豆合作社 / 104
城墙客栈 / 25
串府 / 22
创可贴T恤 / 41

D 得着小馆 / 49
东城区第二图书馆外借处 / 128
东方尚书 / 61
钓鱼台雍和酒店 / 82
都江源 / 30
都一处 / 124
杜革四合院酒店 / 39

G 古槐苑 / 26
古巷贰拾号商务会所 / 46
古韵坊怡景酒店 / 45
桂公府 / 115

H 涵珍园国际酒店 / 37
合家立四合院 / 64
红宝鼎餐吧 / 33
红江湖餐厅(小云南) / 21
红墙史家花园酒店 / 118
红云阁龙腾酒店 / 75
胡同仁庭院酒店 / 48
花家怡园(八爷府·花家店) / 91
花家怡园·四合院店 / 96
皇家粮仓 / 100
皇家驿栈·前门店 / 125
皇家驿栈·天安门店 / 18
惠量小院 / 77

J 吉庆堂宾馆 / 58
江湖酒吧 / 36
交换商店CHANGE / 71
金色凉山 / 56
金台夕照会馆 / 127
金雅会馆(71号院) / 106
京兆尹 / 69
婧园雅筑四合院宾馆 / 119
景山花园酒店 / 24

K 酷虾 / 109

L 老舍纪念馆 / 19
丽江庭院之柔软时光 / 59
利群烤鸭店 / 122
亮点设计中心 / 103
刘宅食府 / 20
侣松园宾馆 / 31

M 马克南四合轩 / 17
猫小院主题咖啡西餐厅 / 55
猫咪咖啡 / 54
茅盾故居 / 44
木棉花酒店 / 16

N 泥庐餐厅 / 81

P 炮局工厂青年旅舍 / 86
朋坐西厨堂 / 73
蓬蒿剧场 / 35
葡萄院儿比萨饼店 / 78

Q 秦唐府七号院 / 47
泉谷酒店 / 126

R 如果客栈 / 52
如是山房 / 74
润琦缘茶馆 / 72

S 圣唐古驿文化创意园 / 85
盛锡福中国帽文化博物馆 / 108
十八茶膳 / 32
16毫米酒吧 / 40
史家胡同博物馆 / 116
束河人家 / 38
死飞 / 70
四合宾馆 / 112

T 天地一家 / 15
天海缘四合酒店 / 102
甜园国际青年旅舍 / 107
TRB / 23

W 王家客栈 / 110
文宇奶酪 / 43
未名四合院精品酒店·宝钞店 / 57
吴裕泰内府菜·东直门店 / 97
五十六号院私房菜 / 76

X 昔巷怀旧主题餐厅 / 63
细活里 / 117
祥福食府 / 93
小院客栈 / 113
新红资客栈 / 101
醒觉咖啡 / 90

Y 壹条龙饭庄 / 123
怡尔国际商务会馆 / 14
乙十六·地坛中心店 / 68
翼栈 / 94
印格时光 / 80
雍和国际青年旅舍 / 92
阅微庄四合院酒店 / 111
云洱小镇 / 62

Z 咂摸餐吧 / 34
藏红花西餐厅 / 79
早春二月新川菜 / 53
紫地客栈 / 42

Index

A
- Aimo Town / 84
- Alley Hotel / 113
- Argo / 73

B
- Backhome Courtyard View Hotel / 64
- BaiHe Vegetarian Food / 95
- Baoyue Restaurant / 60
- Beijing Guxiang 20 Hotel / 46
- Brian Mckenna @ The Courtyard / 17

C
- Cat Theme Cafe / 55
- CHANGE / 71
- Chuanfu Restaurant / 22
- City Walls Courtyard / 25
- Cool Shrimp / 109
- Courtyard 7 / 47

D
- Dezhe Restaurant / 49
- Dongcheng District Second Library / 128
- Dongfang Shangshu Art &Leisure Courtyard / 61
- Double Happiness Courtyard Hotel / 111
- DuGe Courtyard Boutique Hotel / 39
- Duyichu Restaurant / 124

E
- 18 Garden / 32

F
- Former Residence of Mao Dun / 44
- Free as a Bird Restaurant & Bar / 94

G
- Golden Liangshan / 56
- Grand Hotel Du Palais Rouge / 75
- Guigongfu's Mansion / 115

H
- Haloing the Past Theme Restaurant / 63
- Han's Royal Garden / 37
- Hangongque Tea Cafe / 72
- Happy Dragon Courtyard Hostel / 102
- Hongbaoding Restaurant / 33
- Hongjianghu Restaurant / 21
- Hotel Cote Cour Beijing / 114
- Hotel Kapok Beijing / 16
- House of Shuhe / 38
- Hua's Courtyard Fine Dining Restaurant / 91
- Hua's Courtyard Restaurant / 96
- Huiliang Yard / 77
- Hutongren Courtyard Hotel / 48

I
- Imposto Pizza / 81
- Imperial Granary / 100

J
- Ji House / 58
- Jianghu Bar / 36
- Jingshan Garden Hotel / 24
- Jingyuan Courtyard Hotel / 119
- Jinya Hotel / 106

K
- Kingsjoy / 69

L
- Lama Temple Youth Hostel / 92
- Lao She Memorial Hall / 19
- LD Design Center, LDDC / 103

- Life is Elsewhere / 80
- Lijiang Club of Soft Time / 59
- Liqun Roast Duck Restaurant / 122
- Liu's Restaurant / 20
- Lvsongyuan Hotel / 31

M
- MU HOTEL / 45

N
- N.E. Hotel / 110
- NATOOKE / 70
- No.56 Courtyard / 76
- No.44 Cat Theme Cafe / 54
- Noble Club-16 / 68

P
- P.LOFT Youth Hostel / 86
- Peking Yard International Hostel / 105
- Penghao Theatre • Cafe / 35
- Plastered T-shirts / 41
- Purple Courtyard / 42

R
- Red Capital Residence / 101
- Red Wall Garden Hotel / 118
- Rushi Shanfang / 74

S
- Saffron Restaurant / 79
- Scholar Tree Hotel / 26
- Sheng Xifu Museum / 108
- Shengtang Guyi Cultural Creativity Park / 85
- Shijia Hutong Museum / 116
- Sihe Courtyard Hotel / 112
- Siif Design Hotel / 52
- 16mm Bar / 40

- SLOWLANE / 117
- Source / 30
- Spring Trees Restaurant / 53
- Springs Valley / 126
- Sweet Garden House / 107

T
- Taste Restaurant / 34
- TRB / 23
- The Diaoyutai Beijing Lama Temple Hotel / 82
- The Emperor • Tiananmen Branch / 18
- The Emperor • Qianmen Branch / 125
- The Hot Bean / 104
- Tiananmen Best Year Courtyard Hotel / 14
- Tiandi Group / 15
- TouchWoman Cafe / 90
- Trainspotting Restaurant / 83

V
- Vineyard Cafe / 78

W
- Weiming Courtyard Hotel • Baochao Branch / 57
- Wenyu Cheese / 43
- Wuyutai Family Cuisine • Dongzhimen Branch / 97

X
- Xiangfu Restaurant / 93
- Xizhao Temple Hotel / 127

Y
- Yitiaolong Restaurant / 123
- Yun'er Town / 62

审图号：京S（2014）001号

策　　划：刘　权　景晓莉　徐　也
责任编辑：景晓莉　何　玲

图书在版编目（CIP）数据

皇城脚下四合院：北京百家精品四合院旅游指南：汉英对照／北京市东城区旅游发展委员会编. --北京：旅游教育出版社，2014.1

ISBN 978 – 7 – 5637 – 2640 – 0

Ⅰ.①皇… Ⅱ.①北… Ⅲ.①旅游指南—北京市—汉、英②北京四合院—介绍—汉、英 Ⅳ.①K928.91②TU241.5

中国版本图书馆CIP数据核字（2013）第103807号

北京百家精品四合院旅游指南
皇城脚下四合院
北京市东城区旅游发展委员会　编

出版单位	旅游教育出版社
地　　址	北京市朝阳区定福庄南里1号
邮　　编	100024
发行电话	（010）65778403　65728372　65767462（传真）
本社网址	www.tepcb.com
E - mail	tepfx@163.com
印刷单位	北京利丰雅高长城印刷有限公司
经销单位	新华书店
开　　本	889毫米×940毫米　1／16
印　　张	8.5
字　　数	92千字
版　　次	2014年1月第1版
印　　次	2014年1月第1次印刷
印　　数	1—33000册
定　　价	78.00元

（图书如有装订差错请与发行部联系）